God's Global Grace Movement

Hope Rising From An Awakening
in India

David Witt

God's Global Grace Movement
Hope Rising from an Awakening in India
David Witt

All scriptures used are from the JUB or ESV unless otherwise noted. The Jubilee Bible® (JUB®) Copyright © 2013 by Ransom Press International, All rights reserved. The Holy Bible, English Standard Version® (ESV®) Copyright © 2001 by Crossway, a publishing ministry of Good News Publishers. All rights reserved. ESV Text Edition: 2016

Cover Layout: Mark Stafford, Ablaze Media
Editor: Michelle Rayburn, Jeremiah Philip, Becca Timm
Layout: Martha Jaramillo R., Russell Stendal Jr.

For More Information Contact:
SOM International
PO Box 101 Clarkdale, AZ 86324
contact@spiritofmartyrdom.com
www.SpiritofMartyrdom.com
928-634-1419

Printed in the United States of America

RansomPress@outlook.com
Ransom Press International
4918 Roosevelt Street
Hollywood, FL 33021

Paperback: 978-1-64765-059-9
eBook: 978-1-64765-060-5
10   9   8   7   6   5   4   3   2   1

Share Your Comments and Questions:
SOM International
PO Box 101 Clarkdale, AZ 86324
contact@spiritofmartyrdom.com
www.SpiritofMartyrdom.com
928-634-1419

Review this book on Amazon and share with others via social media.

Subscribe to David Witt's Podcast:
AtRiskRadio.com

Receive Free Global Newsletter:
www.SpiritofMartyrdom.com

This book is dedicated to my beautiful bride, Cindy. (My nickname for her is BB.) She is the co-founder of SOM International and for years has labored sacrificially for the global church. Cindy has blessed the ministry with her gift of editing as she has selflessly helped SOM International convey the true beauty of God's people. Her servant heart is contagious and the love of Jesus shines brightly through her. I am truly a blessed man and thank God for the grace I have been given with almost three decades of marriage to Cindy. Thank you Cindy for your tireless dedication to the global work. We love you more than words can say.

-David Witt

Contents

Special Foreword

By Pastor Singh

Brother David Witt has deep wisdom from the Lord. He has traveled to more than fifty-five countries for Christ's mission. Over several decades, he has experienced the church-planting mission and vision. His international experiences of persecution have developed within him a need to represent a global, Christ-centered discipleship-planting movement. He discerned to start writing this book after twenty-one days of special prayers, fasting, and intercession around the world, which was initiated by Spirit of Martyrdom–India (SOM–India). He has a wonderful, godly wife, beloved Sister Cindy. She is a mighty woman of God standing behind the whole global network of Spirit of Martyrdom International (SOM International). They have two children: Jonathan (married to Ally) and Kaitlyn (she also has an Indian name, Mahima, that means "God's glory").

Brother David is like an elder brother to me as well as to thousands of discipleship planters. He is a true, passionate, kingdom-minded man whose love for the Lord is unique. I am Singh, the pastor and founder of a discipleship-planting movement in India. My family and I have the great pleasure and honor to serve together in the global kingdom work. As you read this book, you will capture God's heart for the lost and find inspiration for growing as a global Christ-like leader.

Endorsements

The power source of the persecuted church is not its ability to overcome opposition for the sake of Christ. Instead, dependence on Christ alone fuels the body of Christ to proclaim the gospel in the world's most unreceptive and hostile regions. *Awakening in India* demonstrates that obscurity and meekness are tools with which God equips his children to best demonstrate his glory. I pray the powerful testimonies of transformation that fill the pages of this book will encourage every reader to seek first his kingdom and his righteousness. From this position, we can then begin to grasp how persecution is used by God to bring about the very things he planned well in advance of our time.

—Floyd A Brobbel, CEO, The Voice of the Martyrs, Canada

David's wonderful heart and first-hand experience of the revival that is exploding across India are evident through the pages of this must read, in-depth account of God's power and grace.

—Lindsey Spaethe, managing partner, Eternal Management Solutions/100 XR Ventures

For the past twenty years, I've been celebrating the growing church in the Middle East. Awakening in India is more evidence that the Holy Spirit is drawing people from all backgrounds, tribes, and nations in these latter days. Read the book and be encouraged by yet another great sign among the emerging global church.

—Joel Richardson, *New York Times bestselling author, speaker, filmmaker*

The church planting ministry in India exemplifies the heart of God like nothing I've experienced in my fifty-two years of being a Christian. The truth of identifying Jesus as our pastor/teacher will transform you into a disciple-maker as you read testimonies of the church-planting ministry currently evangelizing all of India in a profound way. . . Be prepared to have your heart challenged and blessed as you read the pages of this account of God's way to win and make disciples.

—John Mahon, *co-founder and board vice president of SOM, USA*

We highly recommend this powerful book, written with simplicity for all cultures to understand-Testimonies declaring faith, love, and hope in the gospel of the kingdom. A must-read for all!

—Larry & Janet Blair, *biblical teachers and leaders*

David Witt has been a close ministry associate for many years. He is, in many ways, a pioneer ready to follow the Lord along new paths to avoid the stagnant ruts that humanistic over-controlled organizations have left in their wake. This was also the case with David's close friend and mentor, Richard Wurmbrand.

Small beginnings have blossomed over the past ten or twelve years into unprecedented results all over the world on a shoestring budget. This is because the presence and glory and conviction of God have been readily evident.

David does not seek to make up his own strategy or programs. Rather, he is willing to travel the world seeking to join in with what God is doing. To participate in what God is doing requires someone with clean hands, a pure heart, and who has not taken God's name in vain nor sworn deceitfully (Psalm 24:4). This is the calling of David Witt and SOM.

—Russell Stendal, author and missionary

Awakening in India is a fresh reminder of God's powerful plan for the end days. This book will challenge your spirit to a new awakening and allow us to commit ourselves more to the Lord's work in these times. You will experience the love of Christ through the testimonies, which will bring much hope and joy to any weary soul. Truly a book that will bring revival and ambition for the Lord's work.

—Humberto M., SOM Mexico director

Introduction

More souls in history have been won to Christ through little, unknown Christians than the sum total of well-known evangelists such as Dwight Moody, William Booth, Charles Finney, Hudson Taylor, Billy Graham, and others. Pastor Singh exemplifies this idea. Only God knows how many tens of thousands of Indians have received Christ through the ministry of Pastor Singh's direct preaching. More profound is the fact that he is not about promoting his preaching and ministry. Pastor Singh is a man who is passionate about training other little people to become faithful discipleship planters to build God's community. Over the past seven years, God has used Pastor Singh to train up over five thousand planters of God's Word; these workers have helped establish over forty thousand fellowships in unreached villages. The impact is 850,000 plus souls won to Christ in nine short years. Though they are unknown names in India, they are known to God.

I desire that this book brings much encouragement during these difficult days around the world. Keep in mind, as you read these stories, how the Indian Christians flourish in spite of the current anti-Christian political leadership. In this Indian network, the gospel has acted as a greater contagion during the pandemic of COVID-19. This group represents a powerless societal minority, where poverty is the rule. These Christians lack technology. Yet with all these challenges, the body of Christ with clean hearts in India is not only overcoming but thriving. I hope the body of Christ in America is infused with what God can do even in the midst of difficulty.

How do the latter days of God's redemptive history and a rural discipleship-planting movement correlate? I believe this book shows they correlate greatly when the reader's eyes are open to the biblical lens of God's end game. I invite you, the reader, to consider this unique report regarding the movement of Indians coming to Christ, and then decide for yourself whether this represents biblical fulfillment. Many end-times books focus on God's judgment of the wicked. Much of latter-day Scripture encourages God's people with promises of a coming grace, victory, overcoming faith, joy, hope, and abundant love.

Consider this quick summary of the character adornment of the body of Christ right before Christ's return: (1) God's people will evangelize every nation, tribe, and tongue (Revelation 14); (2) God's people will gain understanding and will shine like stars – which is a biblical metaphor of messengers of God to all of humankind (Daniel 12); (3) God will pour his Holy Spirit on all flesh, including prophecy, dreams, and visions (Joel 2); (4) The children of the Lord will be righteous, and all these things will be done quickly (Isaiah 60). (Keep in mind the biblical definition of "the church" is God's people, not a building or organization.); (5) God's congregation will be holy (Isaiah 62); (6) The people of the Lord will demonstrate miraculous signs, have authority over demons, and will lay hands on the sick and heal them (Mark 16).

Scripture declares God's desire and fulfillment for a mature bride of Christ. The Lord desires that no one will perish (2 Peter 3). Therefore, God is not satisfied until his people have proclaimed the gospel everywhere, to all people. The Word says that the Lord's favor and grace is upon the poor in spirit, the persecuted, the humble, the oppressed, orphans, widows, and the broken (Matthew 5; Matthew 18; Luke 4; James 1; Psalm 34). Indeed, the people of India represent the greatest proportion of hurting and lost people. Also, speaking of the last days, Jesus proclaims that *the first shall be last, and the last first* (Matthew 20:16).

Today, India is the least-reached nation on earth to access the gospel of Jesus Christ. It is soon to become the most populated (1.4 billion people) and contains some of the most impoverished people groups in the world. Therefore, the Lord's dramatic outpouring of renewal in India is a biblical and historical fulfillment of this. The Lord is raising the least to be global leaders, making those of the past who considered them little people of the world (in power and stature) to become some of the greatest spiritual influencers. As you will discover in the reading of this book, SOM–India has trained and commissioned nearly five thousand missionaries in just over nine years. This figure is from only one Christian network with which SOM International works, and God is doing many other works in other Indian Christian networks.

The example and leadership of this Indian network have been a catalyst to start discipleship-planting networks in sharing God's grace in other parts of Asia, North Africa, Latin America, and North America. We will discuss more of these end-time grace-filled activities in chapter 15. Even if this report of what is happening in India does not meet your "end-times litmus test," then I promise you will be inspired by God's supernatural move in the stories of transformed lives in remote villages of India. There are Christian leaders who believe there is one last great worldwide revival left during which the Lord will fulfill all his biblical promises. If this is true, then India can be the beginning embers of a global revival fire.

Chapter 1

Little People and Big Faith

In 2008, when we founded Spirit of Martyrdom International as a non-profit corporation, I was contemplating where the Lord would call us to serve. When India crossed my mind, I remember thinking, "SOM International should not work in India. It is a black hole of spiritual and physical needs that are too vast for our little ministry." As India's work has exploded, we have discovered God's sense of humor, and I am reminded of my initial aversion.

In 2010, the Lord unexpectedly connected me to a pastor who told me how he was a "little man." Pastor Singh boasts of his small stature and tells others about how in India this is an advantage because he fits comfortably in rickshaws, buses, and trains, and he can sleep anywhere. He also points out how he grew up with little status, being born into the lower caste and a very poor family. Pastor Singh says God is more glorified in him because of his weakness; Christ is highly exalted. Today, I'm humbled and honored to call Pastor Singh one of my closest friends and confidants as we journey together on this path. To me, Pastor Singh is a little man with a big faith.

In the fullest sense, what God is doing in India is a continuation of Holy Spirit growth as recorded in the book of Acts. The gospel is preached in Indian villages where they have never heard the name of Christ. The sick and dying are being healed, demons cast out, and addicts set free. Indians, enchained in the fear of idolatry, superstition, and devout religious practices are finding freedom and joy. Just as beautiful is the pure faith of the Indians who now report their personal relationship with Jesus and the discernment demonstrated in hearing God's voice as they obey his Word. Succinctly put, God is transforming this segment of Indians in radical ways.

The numbers are impressive. In nine years, this network of believers has grown from thirty-five Christian fellowships to over forty thousand! They started with only eight discipleship planters and now have over five thousand. In 2011, SOM–India launched its first discipleship-planting school, and now we have expanded to twenty schools in seventeen states. In 2012, we started the Lighthouse discipleship and sewing schools with ten widows, and now over fifteen hundred women have graduated and started microbusinesses in remote villages. They sew garments and disciple other women. In all this work combined, we estimate that nearly a million Indians have put faith in the Lord Jesus Christ and walk in obedience to their Lord and Savior. Consequently, this network is currently one of the fastest-growing church planting movements in the world! We rejoice that there are other networks, and God is moving in many places.

Possibly the most profound and encouraging feature of what God is doing in India is Pastor Singh's insight of God exalting little people to accomplish his big work. In the end, God gets more glory this way. The Bible shows the pattern of using little people similar to the orphan Moses, the slave Joseph, the ruddy redheaded shepherd David, and the ordinary fisherman Peter. Likewise, this network of Indian believers is made up of little people with little wealth and who are perceived to have little power. They are mostly of a low-caste (Dalit) Hindu background but now have grown to include Muslim, Buddhist, Sikh, atheist, and cultural Christian background believers. Little money, little social status, and little education are the common characteristics of those in this network. Most growth has taken place in remote villages and not the populated cities: little people in little places.

The Lord continues to build a community of like-minded little people working in collaboration. A small Romanian ministry recently joined in supporting the discipleship-planting work in India. This ministry is made up of mostly little pastors who live by great faith in remote villages of Romania. These village pastors have raised funds for sewing machines, bicycles, and for assisting the Indian missionaries with planting disciples in unreached villages. A few pastors raised their support to visit the Indian work during graduation times, but most of these pastors have never traveled outside of Romania. The Romanian congregations have joined in unity of spirit with prayers of intercession.

Pastor Singh's supporting ministry in this growing network of discipleship planters in the USA is Spirit of Martyrdom International (SOM International). SOM International supports this movement in India with the assistance of funds and encouragement as possible.

SOM International is a little organization by the world's standards and a newcomer, having been established in 2008. A small town in Arizona is the base for the ministry. Through it all, I have discovered that God loves little people from little places; it gives him great glory. In my life, I've discovered I readily identify well as a little person in the hands of a big father.

Sabina Wurmbrand was the co-founder of The Voice of the Martyrs global organizations. She was a Christian of Jewish/Romanian background and suffered much for her faith in Christ during the Communist rule of Romania, even enduring a labor camp for three years for not denying Jesus. Sabina and her husband, Richard Wurmbrand, had more impact in serving Christians in the persecuted regions of the world than anyone I have ever known. Once when I was visiting her home with friends, we asked for her wisdom in solving a difficult problem facing in the ministry. After a moment of thoughtful silence, she said, "Ask the little people; they often have your answer."

Sabina exemplified this lifestyle. She loved everyone and especially valued the little people. I have learned the beauty of being a "little" person in Christ and loving the little people as Christ loved them, and even seeking the little people's wisdom. Everyone who comes into the kingdom must come as a child.

With 1.3 billion people currently, India will, within the decade, surpass China, the most populous nation in the world with 1.4 billion people. I'm writing this from a narrow perspective of my understanding based on my experiences. The stories shared in this book are from the narrow, keyhole view of eighteen visits to India, interviews with dozens of Indians, a deep friendship with Pastor Singh, and the treasures that the Lord has revealed to me in his Word. I hope to give you a glimpse into what I have seen the Holy Spirit do among a precious segment of India's people during these past nine years. How long this wave of the Holy Spirit's moving will last in this Indian network, only God knows. For now, I will boast about what the Lord is doing.

To put things in perspective, let me give you some spiritual context of India to help you appreciate the transformed lives presented in this book. India is considered the least-reached nation to the gospel in the world. According to the Joshua Project, India has 2,276 unreached people groups (unreached is defined as less than 2 percent evangelical Christian). By the numbers, this means 1.2 billion people are not experiencing the gospel impact, and over half a million villages in India have no Christian witness.

Nationalism in India is on the rise and boasts nearly one billion Hindus. Fundamentalist Hindus call for the purification of their nation and want India to cleanse the country of all Christians, Muslims, and other non-Hindus. As a result, the persecution of Christians is increasing. Worsening yearly since 2016, India ranked tenth in the world in 2020 for the persecution of Christians. Undoubtedly, the SOM–India network has felt the heavy hand of persecution with two discipleship leaders murdered in 2017. These friends becoming martyrs is a sober reality check for the SOM–USA delegates and I, as we were honored to meet and commission both of these leaders at their respective graduation ceremonies.

The persecution of Christians in India has helped define, mold, and sanctify this movement. Pastor Singh often shares that the unifying force within this network of planters of God's Word is a martyrdom spirit. In this book, you will hear many stories illustrating this kind of faith. Pastor Singh is the founder of SOM-India, and this spirit of faith over fear is a mark of Christ that connects us globally. I hope to highlight testimonies of what God is doing and provide biblical foundations for this work. We have changed the names and do not mention specific locations for security reasons. May these stories and biblical insights encourage you in faith and in your calling to be Christ's witness.

Chapter 2

God Loves the Little Man

Singh is the only son born to an impoverished family from a remote village in India. At the age of fifteen, a medical doctor diagnosed Singh with liver disease, and his prognosis was death within the year. Singh could not eat and keep his food down. Often, drinking water would make him vomit. He became so weak that he could not walk or even sit up in a chair. He could only lie down. Singh neared death more every day, which ruined his father's dream of his son growing up to provide for his family and continue their lineage. His father felt shame for having a sickly boy and turned this shame into anger. He told Singh how worthless he was, saying how he wished his son had never been born.

Singh felt these stings of bitterness from his father but did not respond to his father's anger. In weakness, he had no power and little hope. Spiritual darkness and the feeling of death hung over this small home – one with dirt floors and a grass roof. Singh's mother was uneducated but not one to give up on her son. In desperation, she transported Singh in a cart to visit shrines and religious priests to seek healing. What little money she had, she gave to the holy men to perform their rituals, and she did the prescribed sacrifices, worship to idols, and prayers. The village medicine practitioners gave her son natural plant supplements with prayers for healing. Nothing worked, and money ran out as Singh's sickness continued to progress.

One morning, his mother met a visiting businessman in their village. In a conversation with this man, she mentioned the condition of her son. The Christian businessman encouraged her to pray to Jesus and only Jesus. "Jesus can heal your son," he told her.

Singh's mother arrived home and went to the couch where Singh lay, and she prayed. "Jesus, I hear you are a miracle doctor. Please have mercy. If you heal my son, I will dedicate him to the service of your kingdom for the rest of his life."

Pastor Singh describes this moment as if Jesus had been holding a heavenly cell phone waiting for the call, and he answered immediately. Singh says, "I remember that moment as if it were yesterday. It felt like an instant electric current went through my body." Similar to events in the book of Acts, the Holy Spirit had touched his body. He sat up with an appetite for the first time in one year. He began to feel stronger and was walking around by the afternoon.

After the miraculous healing, the awe of the name of Jesus quickly descended on the hearts of Singh, his father, mother, and younger sister. They wondered, "Who is this God that we have not known, worshipped, or honored? The first time we ask a need of him, this Jesus demonstrates his power so quickly."

The family felt ashamed of the darkness of their hearts as they considered this unknown God, Jesus, his ability to heal. They had only been told the name of Jesus once and that he heals. The weight of their spiritual failure burdened their hearts for two days as they sought to find the Christian businessman who had told them about Jesus. They wanted to ask the man what they should do, now that Jesus had healed their son.

They finally located the man, and he was overjoyed at the miraculous story. He explained the gospel and how Jesus was the Son of God, how Jesus died and rose again for their sins, and they could now become his children and disciples by leaving all other gods and putting their full faith upon Christ alone. The Holy Spirit converted Singh's family, and immediately their guilt was replaced with joy. Singh became an instant evangelist; he went to his neighbors to tell them how Jesus had healed him. There were no Christians in the village to disciple him or churches nearby to visit. The Singh family could not afford to buy a Bible.

For the next three months, Singh would pray and listen to the Holy Spirit. Whatever insight the Holy Spirit would reveal to Singh, he would share and pray with others. Singh finally received his first Bible after three months. Tattered and used, it became a precious gift as he gazed upon the Word of God for the first time. To his delight, he read about the insight the Holy Spirit revealed to him while he was without the written Scripture and Christian guidance. It is a life lesson that Singh will never forget – Jesus is the Word of God and writes his Word upon the hearts of his children.

At sixteen years old, Singh left home to evangelize the villages of India. Leaving his village, let alone his state, was a huge step of faith. He left home with only the clothes on his back, 150 Indian Rupees (about three US dollars), and an old tattered Bible. But he carried faith and courage in abundance. For ten years, Singh walked the length and breadth of India. He estimates that he walked over forty thousand miles during this season of life.

In every village he entered, Singh asked, "Have you heard of the name Jesus?"

Often village people replied, "We have not heard of this person. Maybe you can find him in the next village."

Singh would then simply share his story of how he had been dying and was healed when his mother spoke the name of Jesus. He then would share the life, death, and resurrection of Jesus Christ and ultimately invite others to put their faith upon Christ alone. Everywhere he went, he looked for people with problems. As he found people with physical, emotional, financial, and spiritual problems, he would pray for them. Sometimes, the Holy Spirit would touch these people immediately. Other times, people would track him down later in different villages and tell him how Jesus had healed them of their ailments.

Since Singh had no congregation or mission to support him, his daily provision was always a matter of faith. Singh says that faith was not hard for him. No one had ever taught him to doubt God's provision. The Holy Spirit had discipled him. He read the stories of God's faithful provision in the Bible and, therefore, simply obeyed and trusted the Lord for every meal, drink, transport, health need, and lodging.

Singh remembers days when he was hungry and would come to a mango tree with fruits hanging high. He would command in the name of Jesus for the tree to share its fruit. Immediately, mangos fell to the ground! At night, he would trust the Lord for a safe spot to lie and sleep. Singh likes to joke about how God often gave him a king-sized bed under the trees. He slept in alleys, back yards, train stations, courtyards, and just about anywhere he could find.

In some villages people would view Singh's preaching about Christ as a threat, and they would chase him away with sticks and stones. He estimates that he was chased with sticks out of over two hundred villages during this season of his life. In other villages, people listened to his preaching as their sicknesses were healed. They treated Singh as a holy man. The contrast of being viewed either as a rogue pariah or a spiritual celebrity became a daily reality.

A couple of years ago, during one of my visits to India, Pastor Singh and I visited a village where there was a recently established home fellowship. One of the traditions of India is to give special visitors a garland of flowers. As Pastor Singh and I entered the humble home packed with at least thirty Indians, they welcomed us by placing garlands around our neck. Pastor Singh greeted the fellowship, "In my life, I have entered many villages in the name of our Lord Jesus Christ. Some villagers greeted me with flowers, others have greeted me with rocks. I prefer flowers."

Singh has a natural gift for learning languages. During these years, he hated using translators to communicate, as he called it, "the precious Word of

God." Therefore, in each region he visited, he would spend time learning the local dialect. Currently, he is fluent in seven languages and knows many phrases in other Indian dialects. Little did Singh realize how God would use these experiences of India's cultures, regions, and languages to help launch a national discipleship-planting movement.

In many ways, the grace of God educated Singh. During his younger years, his sickness prevented him from regular attendance at school. Later, his travels, spanning ten years of living by faith, did not afford the opportunity of formal education. He moved daily to another village to preach the gospel. He gained knowledge and understanding easily. During his last few months in his home village before leaving at age sixteen to preach throughout India, he completed and passed his high school equivalency exam. Unfortunately, his family did not have the funds to pay the high school certificate fee to register his completion. In 2001, a seminary offered Singh the opportunity to complete his Bible degree at its school. To be admitted, Singh was able to obtain a high school diploma and pass his college entrance exam. He was offered a scholarship for tuition, but finding room and board was a matter of faith.

Singh has thanked the Lord that he is a little man because he doesn't eat much. Most days, his nutritional intake was rice and *daal* (cooked lentils). The school gave him a cleaning job. Again, Singh rejoiced at the Lord's provision of a job cleaning the showers and bathrooms. He used the remains of the soap to shower and would squeeze discarded toothpaste dispensers for his oral hygiene. All of this did not strike him as a great hardship since the Lord had trained him well in over ten years of homeless living by faith during his preaching ministry throughout India.

In 2003, Pastor Singh's family arranged for him to marry. Singh's wife had received faith in the Lord Jesus at the age of fourteen, and she had prayed to marry a missionary! The first questions Singh asked his wife when he met her were: "Are you willing to sleep on the street or under a tree? Are you willing to trust God for your daily food? Are you willing to be persecuted, arrested, and mistreated? As a missionary, you must trust God for everything."

She answered with a kind smile, "Even some of my relatives think I should marry someone else, but the Holy Spirit has shown me that you are the man for me." As they have suffered together for the gospel, their marriage has grown stronger.

They didn't have enough money to buy rings for their wedding, so they decided to exchange Bibles. They received some funds for their honeymoon. Instead of spending those funds on a comfortable first week of marriage, they chose to spend their honeymoon in a ghetto area to spread the love of Jesus. Singh shares that both of them were so in love with Jesus that their honeymoon was full of joy as they loved and served the children of the ghetto.

One time early in their marriage, Singh and his new bride were praying for food. As they prayed, they heard a "thud" coming from the back yard. Twelve mangos had fallen from the tree. They have learned that God provides for their daily needs. There were times when they received funds, and instead of using the funds for food, they used them to buy Christian materials first. God's Word is always first in their heart and mind.

One day, the Holy Spirit put a particular unreached village upon both of their hearts for evangelism. The village was far, and the bus ticket was fifty cents. The Lord had provided food and Christian tracts, but they didn't have money for the bus fare. As they prayed, they heard a woman outside say she was buying hair. Singh's wife had been slowly losing hair from anemia for the past year and collected it in a box. She was able to sell her hair for fifty cents (the price for the round-trip ticket)! Once again, they saw God's faithful provision.

In fact, since their faith in Christ began, prayer has been a daily ritual for both Singh and his wife. A day rarely goes by where both miss rising early in the wee morning hours to seek the Holy Spirit for the day. From 2003 to 2010, the Lord led Singh and his wife through a season of praying with much fasting. In heartfelt petitions to the Lord, they asked him to grant them a national Indian missionary ministry to evangelize India's unreached regions. During this time, the Holy Spirit blessed Singh and his wife with a vision to see 100,000 Christian fellowships planted by the year 2021. Biblically, the number 100,000 signifies a vast number and perfection. (For example, any divisions of ten represent God's perfection: the perfect moral law of the ten commandments, the tabernacle was one hundred cubits long, and God shall bless the righteous for a thousand generations.) Certainly, God wants to multiply his people to maturity by 2021, and even beyond, until he returns. For seven years, from 2003–2010, they prayed and fasted for God to provide for a discipleship ministry of evangelism. They had no connection outside of India. Then, in 2010, Pastor Singh received a donated computer.

Singh laughs as he remembers the processing speed of that computer. He would press the power button, go to the market, eat breakfast, and shower by the time the computer powered up. This computer was typical of God's work in Singh's life and of how God used little people, little places, and little things for great work.

One day, Singh felt led by the Holy Spirit to search the internet for "Christian Skype chat," and thousands of names appeared. Singh's eyes landed on "Mrs. B," who so happened to be a SOM partner in Arizona. A dialogue began of sharing hearts, Bible verses, and prayer requests. Mrs. B's lifetime desire was to serve in overseas missions. Debilitating health issues prevented that dream of travel ever to come to fruition and kept her mostly housebound. A year before meeting Singh, Mrs. B had prayed that God would either give her a ministry or take her home. About that time, her family gave her a computer and taught her how to connect with people around the world via Skype. She began to make friends, share the gospel, and disciple people in places such as Algeria, the Middle East, China, Pakistan, and more. After one year of dialogue with Singh, Mrs. B was impressed by his humility and vision. He never asked for money; he only wanted prayers! At that point, Mrs. B contacted me and told me about Singh's vision. We made arrangements for Pastor Singh to meet with me via Skype in January 2011. Singh's story captivated me, and so did his vision of six-month-long discipleship-planting schools to train the students to plant house churches of God's people in unreached villages. With Pastor Singh's vision and an amazing "bang-for-the-buck" kingdom budget of forty US dollars per student per month, which paid for the building rent and food, I realized the potential was so great that SOM would be remiss if we did not at least try to help. The Lord taught me over the years how bigger works of righteousness often start with small steps of faithfulness.

In April of 2011, SOM began funding this vision. The first class started with thirty students, and in November, all thirty students graduated. The school was so popular that we immediately added a second school, which doubled the number in the second graduating class. SOM partner Ward and I were able to attend the second graduation service. It was a great honor for me to address these *living martyrs*. At the end of the service, the graduates stood and recited the words of Revelation 2:10: *Be faithful unto death, and I will give you the crown of life* (ESV). Each graduate had one hand over their throat to represent their death and the other hand lifted up to represent their surrender to God. Children danced to the song "God Loves India, and I Love India Too." We had tears in our eyes as we saw a picture of God building his church in the Indian subcontinent.

In just a little over one year, the Singh family had seen the ministry grow from a leadership of eight to ninety-eight leaders and over 139 churches, growing every week! These faithful leaders were from impoverished backgrounds. Not one owned a car or motorcycle, and few even had a bicycle, yet they were very effective planters of God's Word and disciplers of God's people. They used public transportation. With time, SOM International has been able to contribute bicycles or motorcycles to increase their reach.

Pastor Singh says, "I do not want to build church buildings but to build God's people, transformed into his image." Pastor Singh has been beaten, insulted, and threatened for the gospel work. But because of his fearless faith, many follow in his footsteps, and God is increasing the work exponentially.

In the following chapters, you will read the foundational pavestones that have marked and sustained this revival and movement in India. These are stories of transformed lives and how God is forming little Indians into Christ-like mature giants. Like the epic times in the book of Acts, the example in the book of Acts continues today in India and other parts of the developing world.

Chapter 3

Hearing the Word

Singh's family heard the Word of God, and they believed. Romans 10:17 tells us faith comes through hearing the Word of Christ. John 10 emphasizes that the sheep hear the Shepherd and obey his voice. The discipleship-planting movement and every life being transformed today in India is nothing new. These works are patterns found in Scriptures. What follows is a first-hand account of how the voice of God can transform a life.

Beda's Testimony of Leadership

My name is Beda. I was accustomed to a strong Hindu lifestyle. For several generations, our ancestors faithfully lived and died in Hinduism. Anyone we met who was not a Hindu became our enemy and would never be allowed into our home or village. My family and I had chased out Christians and missionaries with big bats and knives. I would get terribly angry when I saw any Christians. I beat one Christian missionary with rods and sticks. I wouldn't even sit with fellow Christian students during my school days. My family and I were very proud of our Hindu religion, our home, and the many rituals in the generations of millions of gods and goddesses. We thought we had everything we needed in Hinduism.

As I grew older, I got married and had two children. We had a great life for fourteen years of marriage. After some time, I had issues with my wife, I lost my business, and it tore my family apart. Our children were left without care and became homeless. I was addicted to wine and immoral living. I left my village and roamed around wherever I wanted since I was homeless.

I spent most of my time alone in the forest with no peace in my life. When I tried to run away, my parents caught me, tied my hands, and took me to the temple for healing. For several months, priests performed various rituals on me, and to my surprise, nothing changed. The Hindu priests taught me that everything is a god; I asked the plants, stones, rivers, sun, moon, and anything in nature to speak to me. I was miserable and discontent with everything in my life. I began to search deeply for reality. Day by day, I hated myself more, and I desperately searched for peace. I found no hope or purpose for living.

One day, I traveled seven hours toward the oceanside to kill myself. I stayed near the seashore for fifteen days contemplating death. On the fifteenth day, as I was under a small hut, I was unable to control myself any longer, and I said, "If there is any god who knows my struggle, then I should hear his voice. Otherwise, I will jump into the sea and kill myself."

At that very moment, I heard a very real voice speaking to me, "Don't kill yourself. I am your true God, and my name is Jesus. I love you and have a purpose for your life."

With all the rituals I had done to please millions of gods and goddesses, I had never heard such a sweet voice. This voice shook my life and touched me from the inside. I said to myself, "I am trying to kill myself, but here is someone telling me there is a purpose for me to live." The voice filled my heart with great joy and hope for the future.

That evening, I shared with a Christian man I had met about the voice I'd heard. He led me in the prayer of salvation, and I gave my life to Jesus. Later in 2013, I was baptized and joined a house group of people who, like me, had a great love for God and for the lost. The group leader discipled and instructed me in my walk with the Lord. As I continued to enjoy my newfound relationship with Christ, I felt burdened for my villagers who lacked the joy I have in knowing the Lord.

After my conversion, I returned to my village, very obviously as a new person. Once the villagers knew that I gave my life to Christ, I wasn't allowed to stay. My relatives, parents, and villagers warned my wife and children not to associate with me. I prayed for my wife and two children to open their hearts to Jesus. After a short time, the Lord worked in their hearts, and they gave their lives to Jesus. They were also excommunicated from the village.

We stayed as a family in a rented mud hut in another village, working as laborers. At work, we were able to witness to many people about Jesus. A Christian group emerged in that area.

Later, my eldest brother was on his deathbed in our home village. I went to visit him, and he was crying on the bed, asking me to forgive him. I told him I had been praying for him for more than a year, and I loved him, and Jesus loved him too. I prayed for him right then, and he was healed from the viral fever and physical complications.

One day, I very clearly heard that Jesus wanted me to serve him and spread his message to the people in unreached villages. As I shared with my home fellowship, the leader introduced me to the discipleship-planting school opportunity, and I eventually graduated in the seventh class. The Lord equipped me to plant four home fellowships in four different villages. I now have received training tools and a brand-new bicycle. I desire to make a bigger impact as I continue to disciple the surrounding Hindu villages and reach India for Christ. I thank God and my USA brothers and sisters who invested in and prayed for me – that I would reach many lost souls for Christ, plant God's Word, and develop God's people in the Hindu villages.

***

Our brother Beda's story demonstrates the power of hearing God's voice. If we are to summarize the ultimate goal of God's Word, what would it be? A scribe in the Gospel of Mark asks Jesus what the greatest commandment is. Jesus gives us the summary of God's Word and his kingdom: *The most important is, 'Hear, O Israel: The Lord our God, the Lord is one. And you shall love the Lord your God with all your heart and with all your soul and with all your mind and with all your strength.' The second is this: 'You shall love your neighbor as yourself.' There is no other commandment greater than these* (Mark 12:29–31 ESV).

According to the order in which Jesus responds, he commands us to listen and hear first so that we can love God and others! Today, *Hear, O Israel* can be interpreted as "Hear, O community of God's people." It is very interesting to follow the rest of the dialogue between the scribe and Jesus.

The scribe says to Jesus that he is right: the Lord is one, there is none beside him, and we should love him and then others.

Jesus then replies to the scribe, *Thou art not far from the kingdom of God* (v. 34).

Jesus did not say, "You are a son of Abraham"; he essentially said, "You are close."

What did the scribe miss? In summary, Jesus mentioned four essentials to faith: hear, one God, love God, and love others. The scribe missed the important command to hear. It's interesting to note that the word "study" is used only three times in the Bible, and the synonyms of the word "hear" are used over 2,500 times (Jubilee Bible translation).

In 2010, I was blessed to be introduced to the ministry called Simply the Story (STS). The founder, Dorothy Miller, asked me how many stories from the Word of God I could recall accurately without adding anything or subtracting anything. I completely failed as I was so dependent upon the written Word of God that I could not repeat one story. I noticed that Jesus did most of his teaching along the way with his disciples and that Jesus rarely had access to the written Word of God. Jesus hid the Word of God in his heart. Jesus is the Word of God. From this challenge, I immediately decided that I needed to be retrained in the Oral Inductive Bible Study method. I thank God for the tutelage of today's president of STS, Andrea.

The results of my learning from the Simply the Story method, observations made from over twenty years of working in unreached nations that persecute and restrict the Christian witness, and specifically growing in my relationship with Pastor Singh initiated the formation of both the Spirit of Martyrdom's Discussion Discipleship Method (DDM) and the Witness Development Evangelism Method (WDE). DDM and WDE training and the principles are being used in the discipleship-planting schools in Northwest Africa, India, Bangladesh, and Mexico presently. We teach these biblical principles of discipleship and evangelism in our Global Ambassadors training. Our Global Ambassadors training equips Christians to be global leaders and multiply disciples. Our number one rule of discipleship is to **listen**. We listen to God through his Word and love him through trusted obedience; then we listen to others to demonstrate God's love to them.

In the next chapter, we will see how the foundation of hearing God directly impacts the biblical truth that all true Christians are priests of God.

Chapter 4

Priesthood of All Believers

The discipleship-planting revival in India is a reformation of the priesthood of all believers. I often ask people, "Was there religion in the garden before Adam and Eve disobeyed?"

Most people answer, "No."

"Will there be religion in heaven?"

Again, most people answer, "No."

"Well then, where and when did religion begin?"

Most people have no idea. I then share the biblical passage, Genesis 3, regarding the disobedience of Adam and Eve eating the fruit from the Tree of Knowledge of Good and Evil. Let's again consider this passage.

What did the Tree of Knowledge of Good and Evil and the Tree of Life represent? The account in Genesis shows us that Adam and Eve were smart, hardworking, and creative. We are told in Scriptures that Adam named all living things – the animals, and it also implies the plants in the garden. Eve joined him in organizing and chores. Both of them were competent in knowledge of the material world. They did not need these trees for material knowledge.

Where did they gain spiritual knowledge? The passage then reveals that their knowledge of the spiritual world was through their relationship with their Father, God. God walked and talked with them in the garden. Note that God gave them the "law" (Do not eat.) orally and in the context of their relationship. (The Lord had the law of Moses written down much later.) The Tree of Knowledge of Good and Evil represented the choice to gain moral knowledge through their own wisdom and self-righteousness judgment instead of God's judgment. Therefore, symbolically, this tree represents the law of God. Later, the Word of God tells us that the law of God brings death, just like eating from the Tree of Knowledge of Good and Evil.

In the bigger picture, the Tree of Knowledge of Good and Evil represents all religions and man's attempt to find self-righteousness. Here in Genesis, we find the spiritual roots of Judaism, Hinduism, Islam, Atheism, and every other religion in the world, including Christianity. The Torah, the Bible, the Quran, the Hindu Vedas, and all other "holy" books are just more "good and bad" fruit on the tree. If you are interested in diving much deeper into this passage of Scripture, consider joining our Global Ambassador training. You can find more information on our website: **www.SpiritofMartyrdom.com**.

Christianity can be one of the worst abusers of this spiritual knowledge tree. Historical Christian institutions that based salvation on the organized church, intercession through priests, and works for salvation were man's religious effort to define and control the knowledge of good and evil. Christian organizations are often guilty of building faith upon their doctrines of salvation rather than upon the Lord of salvation, Jesus Christ. The knowledge-of-good-

and-evil-tree fruit picking is an abundant business in every institutional denomination and mission group today, including the non-denominational. Christian self-help books are produced each year by the thousands, presenting all kinds of so-called secret knowledge and practices. Local churches encourage all of their outreaches to be approved and most often conducted upon the church campuses. Discipleship today comes from organized meetings and studying a "discipleship" book to get the how-to of a disciple while often neglecting the heart and fruit of a disciple. Too often these groups lack the intimate relationships of doing life together as exemplified by Christ with his disciples. It is a time for Christians to ask piercing questions. Do we hear directly from God in his living and written Word? Is Jesus our ultimate pastor/shepherd, or do we take directives from earthly leaders? Do we recognize the voice of Jesus, and are we able to discern the voice of Jesus from others?

If the Tree of Knowledge of Good and Evil represents the law and religion, what does the Tree of Life represent? When we look closely at the clues in Genesis 2 and 3, we find that the Tree of Life was abundant, pleasing to the eye, good for food, free from which to take at any time. It brought healing to the body and, therefore, was a vehicle for eternal life. Does any of this sound familiar? Who is this tree?

The New Testament answers this mystery. Christ shows us that he is the Tree of Life and grace. Christ tells us that whoever eats of his flesh and drinks of his blood will have eternal life (John 6:53). Christ gives us a powerful picture of the flesh and juice that is found in the Tree of Life fruit. We also find that he is the Great Physician who heals our diseases (Matthew 9:35). Jesus is the Bread of Life (John 6:48); and has food that the world does not know (John 4:32). Scripture says Jesus came to bring abundant life (John 10:10).

The two special trees in the garden are a powerful metaphor throughout Scripture and a contrast of spiritual well-being. The moral knowledge tree becomes a curse, and the Tree of Life breaks the curse. Moses was told to put the snake symbol on a pole (tree), and when the Hebrews looked at it, they were healed (Numbers 21). Christ continued the metaphor stating that when he is lifted up, all men will be drawn to him (John 12:32). The Messiah's death, hanging from the knowledge of good and evil tree, canceled the law of sin and death and now brings life to those who put faith in the Tree of Life (the life of Christ). It's interesting to note that in Pastor Singh's testimony, he was sustained often by the fruit of mangos and other fruit trees at the command of the Lord. As he listened to the Lord and kept his heart clean, the Lord provided nutrition even in supernatural ways.

God gave Adam and Eve two trees to exercise their faith. Before their disobedience, they didn't know what death looked like since animals didn't die in the garden. In the same thought, they had no immediate reason to eat from the Tree of Life since they would live forever. Why eat from the Tree of Life at all? One strong reason was that it was good fruit, and God their Father invited them to do so. They could choose to eat the Tree of Life fruit out of delight, love, and good faith in their Father.

Why should they not eat from the Tree of Knowledge of Good and Evil? Because their Father said it was bad, and they would cease to exist, whatever that looked like since the man and the woman had not seen death yet. All animals were plant-eaters before the fall (Genesis 1:30). Death and struggle came with their unfaithfulness. Adam and Eve had to believe God's command in faith. When Adam and Eve disobeyed, they dishonored their Father, became faithless, and made themselves self-righteous judges.

Genesis shows us that God wants a direct, intimate relationship with all his children through faith in his love. Religion sets up priests as intermediaries to get to God, whereas Jesus makes us all priests with direct access to the Father. *Ye also, as living stones, are built up a spiritual house, a holy priesthood, to offer up spiritual sacrifices, well pleasing to God by Jesus, the Christ* (1 Peter 2:5).

Therefore, a key part of the discipleship-planting revival in India is God awakening direct access to himself. The majority of Hindus grow up thinking they have to go through priests to appease and worship their gods. These new discipleship leaders have discovered God's amazing love directly to them and through them. God is teaching them to listen to the Holy Spirit to build God's kingdom people. Practically, it means that the discipleship planters are never told which unreached villages they should visit and reach. They are encouraged to fast and pray, asking God to direct their footsteps to the people and places where they should go.

Pastor Singh shares a story of a discipleship planter who started a home fellowship in an unreached village. The local Hindu priest confronted the leader and told him that if he continued meeting in his village, the priest would have the local men chop him up like a chicken. The discipleship planter knew that the Hindu priest was serious and could make this happen, so he was afraid. When talking to the network leadership, someone asked the discipleship planter, "Did the Holy Spirit call you to this village?"

The discipleship planter affirmed that he had heard the voice of God call him.

His leader answered, "Then God will provide and protect you. If God allows for your enemies to kill you, then we will bury you well."

After the discipleship planter was encouraged in his original calling, he remained faithful, and he and the local fellowship continue to prosper there today.

Another discipleship planter is Jamal. He is a good example of the Indian leadership who understand and teach the concept of the priesthood of believers. Here is his story in his own words:

Jamal's Testimony of Leadership

My name is Jamal, and I was healed from a lung disease and gave my life to Jesus. Since the day I was saved, I began actively witnessing the power of the gospel to hundreds of people. I would share the gospel at home, on the streets, in the marketplaces, and wherever I was led to share. As I served the Lord, my passion for the lost continued to increase, and the burden was heavy on my heart. The only thing

I knew to do was regularly fast and pray when I felt such deep brokenness in my heart.

One day, I had a vision about a village, and I heard the name of the village very clearly in my heart. Since I am unschooled, I couldn't figure out the direction to this village from where I was. One fine morning, as I fasted and prayed again, the Lord told me to walk toward the unreached village in a particular direction. I walked about three hours and found the village. At the entrance, I saw the name of the village I'd heard during prayer, and the village looked exactly like I saw it in the vision I'd had. I said, "Yes Lord, this is the village you showed me, and I am right here. Thank you for bringing me here!"

I thanked the Lord and surrendered the village into the hands of God. The very first day, by faith, I laid my hands on a man who was suffering from a fever, and God instantly healed him. A paralyzed man was also healed! It was a great surprise for the village people and for the family of the paralyzed man. They told me to explain how I learned to heal people.

I told them, "I am just a man, but it is Jesus who heals and brings people into his kingdom." I praised God and was filled with great excitement and hope that the whole village would come to know Christ. The people were very accepting of me and were curious to know more about the Jesus I talked about. They were drawn to experience Christ in their lives.

***

The prince of this world ruled this village in social, economic, and political ways. The people had different types of worship systems to multiple deities in hopes to appease the gods and prosper. When there was a drought in the village, people conducted a special worship time to seek the rain god's favor. They would bow down to a carved stone with a picture of a deity and would perform a special marriage ceremony for frogs, expecting the rain god to have mercy and visit the village. They paid homage to fire, wind, water, and all of creation.

The whole village was addicted to wine and would get drunk and fight every day after work. Children and youth lived in a very unhealthy atmosphere and were not cared for by their parents, which had a severe effect on their daily lives and character. Since there was no care from the parents, young children were forced into child labor. Many children became self-centered and finally migrated to the cities, craving the urban lifestyle. Many of them never came back to their parents again. Some got involved in notorious crimes and ended up in prison. The number of children and youth decreased since they didn't want to stay in the village with their parents.

Idol worship and Hindu festivals were a very integral part of their lives. However, today in this village, only a minority perform idol worship. The village temple is lacking devotees.

The gospel entered into this village. The Lord has restored family life! The Christ-filled lives of the parents have transformed the lives of the children and youth. Now whole families sit together in their homes for family time, singing, discussing Bible stories, and having a sweet time of prayer. Instead of quarreling, the family has been filled with sweet love, harmony, deeper relationships, and rejoicing in the Lord. Families are united and not divided. As a result of many prayers, children and youth have come back to their parents and given their lives to Jesus. Many youths have turned away from crime, quarreling, and alcohol abuse. Instead of participating in Hindu temple celebrations, they are celebrating their lives each day with Jesus. There is a vibrant and dynamic congregation meeting going on in this village several times a week.

Families have discovered that the landlords try to encumber them with lifelong debt, bondage, and essentially slavery. The gospel has opened the eyes of the villagers, and many have found freedom from bondage. They no longer borrow money from the landlords; instead, each one tries to live by faith and within their own income. This change of attitude has caught the attention of the landlords because they are losing the cheap laborers. Therefore, they persecute and harass the believers, but joyfully the new Christians live their lives with Jesus. Some of the villagers are blessed to have their own small home-based businesses, providing various services to the community and making their living.

＊

The discipleship-planting revival and movement in India reminds us that when Christ becomes Lord of our lives, we are all priests of his kingdom and, therefore, called to be faithful witnesses.

In the coming chapter, we will hear how these new Indian Christians are now being faithful "priests" and "witnesses" and how rapid multiplication of disciples to the Messiah's community of people is a joyful passion of participation for all the believers. How important is the command of God to make disciples?

Chapter 5

Multiplication of His Image

As an ordained pastor, I have the privilege to officiate at weddings and lead young couples in premarital counseling. I begin all sessions with Genesis 1–3, "What is the first command in Scripture by God?"

The answer: *And God blessed them, and God said unto them, Be fruitful and multiply and fill the earth and subdue it and have dominion . . .* (Genesis 1:28). Christians sometimes misunderstand the importance and context of this first, great command.

Verse 27 gives insight that God made man and woman in the image and likeness of himself. The Word of God reveals that God is spirit and flesh in Jesus. Therefore, to multiply the image of God, we must first multiply the characteristics of the Spirit of God as well as the behaviors of Christ.

What most Christians refer to as the Great Commission of Jesus from Matthew 28 and Mark 16 simply restates and summarizes the first commandment of God in Genesis. With this in mind, consider the words of Christ: *Go ye therefore and teach all nations, baptizing them in the name of the Father and of the Son and of the Holy Spirit, teaching them to observe all things whatsoever I have commanded you; and, behold, I am with you always even unto the end of the age.*

Amen (Matthew 28:19–20). Jesus keeps the continuum of God's heart and Word.

God reveals his glory in the natural order. A rancher values the cows, sheep, horses, etc., that reproduce in large numbers, and a farmer prays for an abundant harvest. Therefore, if the rancher celebrates the new birth of his herd and a farmer rejoices over a plentiful harvest, how much more does God want us to reproduce his glory (i.e., make disciples)?

The vision of one hundred thousand churches is to be built and multiplied by God's provision, and it is for his glory. Similar to Scripture, the discipleship-planting movement in India teaches every believer to multiply. Everything SOM International supports in India is evaluated by how well and quickly it can reproduce. The tools that we give must multiply without us, as patterned in Scripture. For instance, SOM International gives the "tool" of a six-month missionary/discipleship-planting school to each student. We provide funds to rent the room and feed the students. There is no charge for the students to attend the school. During the six months, students learn practical, biblical ministry skills and do outreach together to immediately apply these new skills.

Upon graduation, we do not offer a pastor financial support program. Why? We want discipleship planters to be dependent upon the Holy Spirit and not funds from the West. Some discipleship planters become bi-vocational, while others learn to live by faith, and their planted fellowships offer help to supply their needs. If we were funding discipleship planters, the growth would be limited by funds from the West instead of the unlimited resources from God our Father.

How effective is the Indian discipleship-planting movement becoming in multiplying? Thus far, we have measured a trend that the average graduate will plant five home fellowships within twelve months. An average of twenty people will respond to the gospel and become active participants. After the first year, the discipleship planters will continue to plant more indigenous fellowships with the help of new disciples, so the movement builds momentum.

Another tool that SOM supplies, as funds are available, is a quality bicycle for each discipleship planter. Each bike costs only one hundred dollars. After receiving this tool, we have found that the average discipleship planter can increase his fellowships planted by three more congregations per twelve months than he would without the bike. Considering that a one-hundred-dollar investment brings the yield of sixty more souls in one year is a great kingdom outcome. Multiplication is the principle for giving bikes, and these are not owned nor maintained by SOM–USA.

SOM uses the same multiplication principle for all tools supplied to India, such as a van or car for the ministry, sewing machines for widows to start trade centers, MP3 players for those who cannot read or write, DVDs of the *Jesus Film* and *God's Story*, and many Bibles. These are all tools that can multiply results without our continued involvement. Therefore, if tomorrow SOM-USA is no longer able to assist, the work will continue. It is dependent upon Jesus and not upon SOM International.

Disciples teach multiplication through imitating what we do and say. It's important that every ministry evaluate the demographics of its flock. The pattern of Scripture is that Christ did not ask his disciples to do or say anything that he first did not do or say. Practically, nothing should be done or said that is not possible for the least disciple to imitate.

The Lord started teaching me this principle in the beginning days of this discipleship-planting movement in India. During one of my visits to an Indian graduation, I brought my iPad that has multiple Bible translations and some great study tools. Unfortunately, I forgot to bring my printed Bible. After teaching the first day with my iPad in a group of over one hundred leaders, the Holy Spirit convicted me of my offense. I realized that I was a model of Christian maturity to these young leaders. Also, these leaders were from very poor households and made an average of fifty dollars a month. There was little hope that these discipleship leaders could purchase an iPad on their own. They mistakenly could have come to these conclusions:

Mature leaders of the church have fancy electronic tools to help them study and teach.

God blesses mature leaders with expensive electronic tools.

Once I get these tools, I can mature to the level of effectiveness of great leadership.

All of these assumptions are, of course, false. However, the little things young disciples see me doing will become an example of a "normal" Christian leader's life. I now teach with a Bible in my hand because I know every discipleship planter has a Bible. The Scriptures are sufficient for discipleship and godly witness.

In the following story, a widowed mother exemplifies the multiplication principle. As you read, keep in mind that Revathi is a house fellowship member and did not graduate from our schools. Financially, she is poor, yet she plants God's Word because of the modeling of a bold witness and the discipleship of her local discipleship planter. Notice what she uses, specifically her own home and even persecution, to help multiply God's Word through her children.

Revathi's Testimony of Leadership

A widowed mother, Revathi, and her two little children gave their lives to Jesus when visiting a home fellowship two hours away from their village. After they accepted the Lord as their Savior, they developed a great love for the lost Hindu villagers. Revathi was deeply passionate and had a great burden for her own village. Revathi's village was tightly closed to the gospel, and its leaders permitted no other religion besides Hinduism. The congregation members prayed with Revathi for several weeks for her village.

As they prayed, the Spirit of God began to stir Revathi's heart. She heard the Lord speaking to her to open her house for the Lord. As she shared, the discipleship planter became excited and joined Revathi along with a few other fellowship members. They began praying once a week in her home. Within four weeks, a few children, men, and women were led to her home church. They believed that Jesus is the only Lord and gave their lives to him.

Revathi's landlord and the villagers protested very strongly against her allowing a fellowship of Christians in her home. They burst into anger and insulted her and her children. They said, "You have deceived us by bringing a new religion to our village, and you have defiled our village." They warned her not to have Christian gatherings in her home or the village.

Revathi continued to pray and seek the Lord. The Holy Spirit revealed to her that God would use her in her workplace, even through the rejection she encountered for his kingdom's expansion. She looked for ways to witness and found a place right outside of her village by a bridge. A major storm with flooding had broken the bridge, and the government had begun to rebuild it. She got a job cooking for the laborers in a small hut beside the bridge.

She would tell Bible stories to the laborers' children as she cooked. The children enjoyed the stories, and a few other women were drawn to her through the Bible stories. The story of the five loaves of bread and two fish increasingly attracted the attention of the children. The Lord began to work in their hearts to surrender their lives to Jesus. Through the children, a few of their family members also gave their lives to the Lord.

The believers met twice a week in Revathi's small hut next to the bridge. She told Bible stories and had prayer times for her village. As she informed the discipleship planter in her area about these things, he rushed there to see the work among the laborers. He shared the Word and prayed with the laborers.

Revathi says, "Though we were not allowed to meet in my house, the Lord has his own way. The roadside broken bridge is a great place for us to meet and worship the Lord. The presence of God is so real. People can't stop the children of God from witnessing and having fellowship to worship the Lord. Our God is not bound to a church building, a house, or any particular place. Anywhere two or more are gathered, the presence of the Lord is there. What a glorious God we have, and we can meet in the Spirit anywhere!"

***

It isn't only the trained discipleship planters but simple village men and women who the Spirit of the Lord empowers to witness wherever he leads. Praise God for the hard work, commitment, and passion of our discipleship planters to empower God's people. The Lord is raising up congregations faithfully witnessing. Thousands of our home fellowships are meeting in houses, by the roadside, under the trees, and under bridges; many meet secretly in restricted villages.

The work in India reminds us of the biblical principle that when God moves in revival, there is fruitful multiplication. Let's pray for the Holy Spirit to continue to fuel a revival fire throughout India that spreads throughout all nations. May we see the day that God's people explode in bountiful abundance with the multiplication of his disciples.

Accepting Christ is just one step of discipleship. The great challenge is to disciple Indians to pattern their lives in the way of Christ. In a land of 1.3 billion people with hundreds of languages, how is discipleship even possible? Let's look next at the beauty of simplicity in the movement of God. The next chapter demonstrates the authority of planting God's Word in God's people when there is only one textbook.

Chapter 6

Word of God: One Textbook

Simplicity is a refreshing mark of this Indian network. It goes back to the basics of faith in God and obedience to his Word. With a plethora of distractions today, the return of pure discipleship has made an all-encompassing ministry impact. Simplicity manifests itself both spiritually and physically, as the focus is faith in Christ and his Word. Combined with obedience to the Word of Christ, it transforms lives.

The discipleship-planting schools have one textbook: the Bible. It's hard to overemphasize this point. We believe that the Word of God is sufficient for discipleship and witnessing. Scripture itself claims this: *But as for you, continue in what you have learned and have firmly believed, knowing from whom you learned it and how from childhood you have been acquainted with the sacred writings, which are able to make you wise for salvation through faith in Christ Jesus. All Scripture is breathed out by God and profitable for teaching, for reproof, for correction, and for training in righteousness, that the man of God may be complete, equipped for every good work* (2 Timothy 3:14–17 ESV).

At the same time, we do not lift up the Bible as an object to be worshipped or as a holy relic. Materially, the Bible is only paper and ink. The Bible records the words of God and, therefore, becomes an instrument to know God the Father's true holiness. The Bible is not the truth in itself but the conduit of revelation regarding the truth of Jesus Christ. The Bible cannot convert people, for only the Holy Spirit makes converts by taking the words off the page and convicting humankind's heart. For the Indian discipleship-planting network, the Bible becomes the central tool to lead others to Jesus and mature them in faith.

The Indian spiritual soil is a dry wasteland. Over 65 percent of Indians live in remote villages. They are poor and lack access to most resources. Most Indians have never heard of Jesus and the gospel message. Most do not even know a Bible exists, let alone have seen one. Most Indians have never even met a Christian. A vast population of low-caste Indians feel oppressed, discouraged, and fearful. Their religious idealism has not worked. Amid this arid spiritual wilderness enters the refreshing water and clarity of God's Word. Shiva's story shows what the Holy Spirit can do when the Word of God empowers a high school dropout.

Shiva's Testimony of Leadership

My name is Shiva. I was born to a poor Hindu family, and my parents and villagers had little care for me. I was unable to remember things, and somehow, I reached high school and then failed to graduate. I felt so worried about my future and began to associate with a very mischievous group.

Day by day, my life was filled with uncertainty of my future, lack of peace, and challenges in my community. One day, I met an evangelist in a market area. He talked to me and showed genuine interest in me. His words were very comforting, something I had never experienced before. He shared with me the hope in Christ. I was filled with deep joy and surrendered my life to Jesus.

He gave me a Bible and encouraged me to read it every day. I began to pray and found that I could remember many things from the Bible. As I fasted, the Lord burdened me with love for the lost and hopeless people in my village and surrounding villages. I felt the Lord calling me to serve him, and I prayed for him to prepare me. The devil tried to discourage me, and I knew entering into a Bible school would not be easy.

I heard about the opportunity to learn the Word at a discipleship-planting school and wanted to enroll to help prepare me for ministry. At the end of six months, I was commissioned for reaching the unreached. I am now blessed with good memory, and in the same village where people didn't care about me, more than twenty-three people came to the Lord and are part of a house group.

***

Shiva's story is one testimony out of many showing how practical, simple training empowers the Indian body of Christ to reach the lost, plant God's Word, and reap his people. There are thousands like this brother who are untapped leaders waiting for the opportunity for training. Please pray for this discipleship-planting movement to start more schools all over the land of India! The Lord is drawing people unto himself through the simplicity in his Word. The disciples plant home fellowships in the unreached remote villages, mountains, and slums.

I have been asked many times how we keep our cost for the schools so low when especially considering the effectiveness. I can summarize the cost and effectiveness in one word: simplicity. The theology and doctrine taught at the schools are practical and transformational. The classes run three days a week at rented offices with plastic chairs. The Indian instructors volunteer their time, and we have one textbook, the Bible.

Here is a breakdown of current expenses:

To support a discipleship planter for one month, it costs 40 dollars. At the end of six months, we have invested 240 dollars. As we already discussed in a previous chapter, the average discipleship planter will see one hundred souls respond to faith in Christ within twelve months. We do not provide any residential schools because that is very expensive. All students commute to school. No discipleship planter ever receives a salary; the funds only provide the tools. Logistically, here are some examples of how we conduct ministry:

1. The school runs three days a week, which leaves the students three days to work and one day of rest.

2. The buildings that house the schools are rented and located in humble places; they are small and would fit fifteen Americans, yet thirty Indians are comfortable.

3. The Indian network of discipleship planters come from impoverished and low-caste backgrounds. Therefore, they are comfortable with simple

classrooms, accommodations, and food. They all serve each other, and there is no need to hire cooks or cleaning staff.

4. The instructors all live by faith. They volunteer their time and are not paid staff. In fact, there is no paid staff in this discipleship-planting school network. Everyone serves and trusts the Lord for their daily provision.

5. There is no advertising budget for the schools because all the students come from established fellowships in the network and are told verbally about the opportunity.

6. Schools are reproduced in strategic locations in India. The schools maintain between three to six instructors, and each school is limited to thirty students.

7. Each student is responsible for his or her own transportation to and from school. Therefore, schools do not have to purchase and maintain vehicles.

8. Since the Bible is the only textbook, the cost of the materials is only the expense of the written Word of God.

You might recall, Pastor Singh received his first Bible three months after he had started preaching Christ. From the age of sixteen, he traveled by faith for ten years through every state in India (1992–2002). He had the written Word of God and the Holy Spirit to disciple him. His formal Bible training was after this decade of preaching and trusting God for his daily provision. When he received his master of theology degree, Pastor Singh shared that the Lord spoke to him and said, "Now that you have learned all this biblical knowledge, I want you to go back to the simplicity of faith that you experienced from the beginning."

In the following chapter, we will see how Indians in this revival follow the biblical teaching of one global body of God's people and one leader over his congregation.

Chapter 7

One Church, One Pastor

P astor Singh likes to say often that the discipleship-planting network in India "does life together." This network works together through relationships rather than through an organization. Love for God and each other is the goal. How do we do this? Jesus is the head, the CEO. He is the pastor.

What they have discovered is God's Word teaches there is one church and one pastor. Therefore, the discipleship planters are not trying to build up an organization; they are trying to build up a movement of people led by God. Most of these caring "pastors" of multiple churches don't even call themselves pastors but prefer the title "missionary." They are building up the fame of Jesus Christ. Church comes from the word *ekklēsia* in Greek. It means "an assembly of God's people together or set apart fellowship." It's a celebration of God's transforming work in the hearts of his people.

In Colossians 4:15, the apostle Paul demonstrates this understanding when he says: Salute the brethren who are in Laodicea and Nymphas and the congregation which is in his house. (JUB). Notice that Paul did not say "house church." There is no focus on the building but only God's people in Nympha's home. Paul continues to refer to the church in the New Testament as the people gathered in a specific place. A right understanding of the church leads to healthy participation. Each person discovers that he is an important part of God's church to keep a healthy growing body. The focus of the church is on relationships with each other and ultimately with God through Jesus Christ; the Holy Spirit's indwelling empowers them.

Jesus said, *I am the good shepherd* (John 10:11, 14). Here, pastor and shepherd are interchangeable in the Greek. Every believer is taught to hear directly from Christ through his Word and Holy Spirit. Believers do not need a priest to connect with God because they have direct access to Christ himself.

Christ, as the head of the church, is an equalizing force. Every leader of the network must submit to his Word and be accountable to the unity working through the plurality of leadership. They also experience the joy of having different roles and yet equality before God in value and love. Peram's story demonstrates how this practice is happening in India.

Peram's Testimony of Leadership

My name is Peram, I was raised in a Hindu family. Both of my parents were from a low-caste family as per the Hindu social structures. Right from my childhood, I learned I was a child born to a low-caste family, and I was not equal to other children in my village. According to the Hindu religious belief, I learned to consider myself lower since I came from the feet of the Hindu gods.

The Hindu philosophy of human birth strongly rules our village. Worship places in our area are allotted according to the higher and lower community structures. When someone dies from our community, we have to carry the dead body to a far place for burial because the landlord believes it would curse him to a lower caste if we held it in his domain. This belief system dominates hundreds of villages. When we fall sick, no doctor will treat us out of fear of being cursed. It's common in our community to beat and abuse women and children. Hundreds of villages in our region suffer under the corruption of the landlords.

When I was a child, I was not allowed to sit with the upper-caste students in school, and we lower-caste students ate our lunch in a separate allotted place. We would not be given official work; we would have to clean the school campus and toilet areas.

I felt deep pain in my heart and did not value my life because of how I was treated. I wondered if there would ever be a way for me to break all my emotional pain and free myself from the feeling of inequality. For many generations, our ancestors died as discriminated against and devalued human beings. In their time, even the shadow of our people was considered unclean.

One day, I met a Christian man who shared with me how Jesus in the Bible stood with all types of people despite their social differences. People who found Christ lived with absolute freedom and enjoyed a new life in Christ. The story of a leper from the Bible caught my attention, and one question struck me: how could an outcast leper be brought back to the community after healing? I could see myself as a leper, and I wanted to be accepted and loved by people in my village. I felt a great need to know this Jesus about whom he spoke.

A few days later, I was convicted of my helpless and hopeless situation without Christ. The great value and hope I could have in Christ became clear to me. With tears streaming down my face, I acknowledged my sins and surrendered my life to Jesus. I joined a Christian group where I experienced the intimacy, respect, and honor they had for each other as true brothers and sisters in Christ.

I no longer feel broken, unequal, and devalued. Instead, I feel I am a child of the God who is Lord over all creation and gives me joy each day. The Lord put a burden in my heart to serve thousands of broken people in my community who live bitter, less valued, and hopeless lives.

As I prayed for a few months, I felt God call me for his ministry, and I felt a need to undergo ministry training. As a result of my prayers, the regional leader of the discipleship-planting school helped me enroll. The training has equipped me with great tools and the power of the Holy Spirit.

I graduated in 2018 and was commissioned. It was a glorious experience in my life. Gathering together with hundreds of brothers and sisters in Christ and celebrating God's great work was a feeling I will never forget. The Lord has already directed me to ten villages in my area, and I covet your prayers.

***

Peram's story demonstrates the power of family. We are one in Christ and have one Father and one pastor, Jesus. We share in the joy of Christ's leadership and inheritance. The next chapter will examine how Pastor Jesus invites us to seek out broken people and heal their hurts.

Chapter 8

What's the Problem?

J esus came for the sick and wicked, not the healthy and righteous. The focus of all discipleship planters, Lighthouse discipleship sewing centers, and the India Christian Network is to seek the lost, hurting, and broken people and share Jesus. Remember that Jesus said he did not come for the healthy but for the sick and for sinners, not for the righteous (Mark 2:17). The gospel is not for successful people but for failures. Jesus surrounded himself with people who had failed in life and sought Jesus alone for life. The Scriptures tell us that *God opposes the proud but gives grace to the humble* (1 Peter 5:5 ESV).

Someone asked Pastor Singh, "When you go village to village with the gospel, what does that look like? Do you just stop on a street corner and begin to speak or stop the first person you come across?"

Pastor Singh replied, "I never know who I will meet, either on the street or corner of the village or along the way, but I go with much prayer that God will bring someone on my way with some problem. It then paves the way for me to talk about Jesus. My conversations begin with one or more problems a person is going through, and then I tell my story and share who Jesus is."

Pastor Singh teaches: seek one, reach one, and teach one. This principle is the heart of their outreach. When discipleship planters enter an unreached village, they pray as they walk, and they look for the Holy Spirit to lead them to someone in need. The leaders seek one person whose problem Jesus can cure. When they meet the person with a need, they reach this one person by listening, responding in kindness, and pointing to Jesus as the answer to their needs. When an Indian responds and is reached by the love of Jesus, the discipleship planter will continue to meet with them regularly to help the new disciple grow as a leader and encourage them to immediately reach others. In this way, they teach them by the Word and by the example of their lives. This example also demonstrates that discipleship and evangelism are not divided; instead, they are one. Disciples share their faith, and evangelists are disciples who look for hurting people to proclaim the good news.

When were the apostles truly converted? It was after the crucifixion and resurrection of Jesus Christ. Acts 2 records the complete conversion of all the disciples. When the power of the Holy Spirit came upon them, this changed their natures and converted them in heart and mind. Most modern Christians will define someone as converted when they believe the gospel and are born again. By that definition, the apostles were un-converted for three years during Jesus's teaching ministry with the apostles. It's common for some organizations to disciple *from* conversion, yet Jesus discipled *to* conversion.

Luke 19:10 says, *the Son of Man came to seek and save the lost* (ESV). He is seeking and saving the lost all over the world. As you continue to read the following testimony, you will be able to see how the Lord seeks and saves his precious people, created in his own image, wherever they are. It's marvelous how Jesus finds people in their lost, broken conditions, and transforms their lives.

Khila's Testimony of Leadership

My Name is Khila, and I am twenty-two years old. I graduated in the eleventh class of discipleship planters. I was born to a fundamental Muslim family and had three older sisters. Both parents were devout Muslims, and each day they practiced the Muslim way of life very closely. My father used to be an extremely violent person, both at home and outside. My sisters and I would hide in fear when we heard our father coming home. He was addicted to drugs and alcohol and lived an immoral life. For work, he drove a vehicle for a rich man who paid him a lot of money for living a sin-filled life. My father took pride in having his boss protect him since his boss was very influential in the social and political realm. My mom would get chased out of our home like a street dog, often beaten or tortured. A few times, my father attempted to pour acid on her to burn her. My mother would hide for days at other homes out of fear of my father.

We starved for many days with no food, and my mother's income was not enough to meet our daily needs. She would call upon Allah with great honor and say special prayers five times a day. One time a non-Muslim woman was pronouncing the name of Mohamad without adding the title prophet. I was terribly angry and forced her to honor Mohamad as Prophet Mohamad.

Day by day, our home became more like hell. One evening, my mother felt so much discouragement that she wanted to kill herself by jumping into the river with her four children. She began to sing to Allah and cried out, "If you exist, please come and give me peace. I need a new way of life or I will kill us all tonight."

That night we experienced a miracle. A Christian sister came to our home from a neighboring village. She said she sensed God tell her to visit our family because we were broken and had a lot of pain.

As a family, we were planning death in the next hour, and this precious Christian sister was like God visiting us. She entered our home, and with her sweet, loving voice, asked us how we were doing. We were all in tears of desperation. She shared how God the Father loved us so much that he sent his Son to die for us. "Jesus died, rose again, and is alive today," she said. "He is the answer to all our problems in life." She asked us to call upon the name of Jesus, and as a family, we called upon him for the first time.

We cried out, "Jesus, we have never called upon your name. We have dishonored and rejected you all of our life. In these last moments of our lives, we want to call upon your name as the living God who speaks." We shouted, "Jesus, save us from this suicide and broken home! Give us peace!"

The dear sister led us in a prayer of salvation.

We cannot explain how glorious and peaceful this moment was in our home. We were filled with so much joy and hope as we were transformed into new people. My father was gone from home for a week during this time. For that week, we prayed relentlessly for his salvation. At the end of the week, the Christian sister brought a pastor to our home to meet my father. It was the first time my father had ever prayed with us; he had a quiet spirit and gave his life to the Lord.

Since that day, God has given him freedom from his old violent habits, and now he lives a holy life following Jesus. The mighty work of Jesus coming to our home in the final minutes before committing suicide was a miracle. Oh, how much he loves us. For the last six years, we have lived with unspeakable joy for the mighty work of deliverance and salvation in our lives.

There were a few Christians with whom we would meet regularly for Bible study and prayer. There is no formal Christian church or gathering in our area. There is heavy persecution toward the minority of Christians who worship Jesus. I have been reading the Word of God for a couple of years, fasting, and praying. The Lord heard my prayers and provided a discipleship planter in our area. It filled us with much joy to have someone who could teach and instruct us in the Word of God. Meeting for fellowship with this brother broke my heart more and more for the lost and confirmed my calling for ministry.

The discipleship planter connected me with the discipleship-planting schools. I enrolled and was deeply encouraged to grow in my faith and relationship with other students. I look forward to serving the Lord the rest of my days and witnessing weekly outreaches.

***

The major mark of Khila's family was brokenness. They were humbled and at the point of suicide. God loves the humble, broken, and poor in spirit (Psalm 34). Why? We will see in this next chapter how God transforms people like this to look just like him. He receives glory when broken people are transformed by his love.

Chapter 9

Transformed People Transform People

Some people tend to think the Good Samaritan's story in Luke 10 is a Sunday school lesson on being a good neighbor; however, the context of the story is salvation. A lawyer stood up to test Jesus and asked, *Master, what shall I do to inherit eternal life?* (v. 25).

When Jesus helped the lawyer understand that to love God and love others is the greatest commandment and standard for eternal life, the lawyer wanted to justify his self-righteousness by asking the question: *who is my neighbour?* (v. 29). The corrupted flesh always strives to find righteousness in its own strength.

This parable shares the gospel. The man who had been beaten represented the "lostness" of mankind. All of humanity is half-dead without the spirit. The flesh must be born again to have eternal life. The robbers represent the evil of the world, Satan, and our flesh. The religious leaders represent the self-righteousness of the flesh trying to make themselves right before man and God. The Samaritan is Christ. Christ comes to the sinful, beaten man who is an enemy of his righteousness and hates God (the Jews hated Samaritans). Christ has compassion on the man's sinful state and binds his wounds, just like Christ binds his church's wounds today with his blood and the Holy Spirit (oil and wine in the story).

The Samaritan takes the man to the innkeeper, who represents God's people very well. In this metaphor, Christ gives provision to the church. The Samaritan instructs the innkeeper/body of Christ to take care of the man until he returns (an excellent metaphor for the return of Jesus Christ).

Every person that becomes a new creation in Christ becomes a good Samaritan. Even Jesus points out that only God is good (Luke 18:19). The benefit of the gospel is that every person has the opportunity to exchange his corrupted flesh for the life of Christ, who represents the Father. The goodness of believers is a fruit of the new life brought by the Holy Spirit abiding in every true Christian. When Christ rules in our life, we can finally become the "good neighbor."

Much of the focus happening in the revival in India is transformation. In many of the interviews I have done with Indian believers, there is a common pattern. They share the growing corruption and "lostness" of their lives. Many of them go through a religious phase of seeking meaning and self-righteousness, only to be disillusioned. Finally, Christ reveals himself through goodness. Then they share how their lives are changed, and they begin to love others.

The following is an interview I did with Sutish. As we listen to his story, we discover that his life represents every character of the Good Samaritan's story.

Sutish's Testimony of Leadership

Sutish was born to a Hindu family, and today he is a believer in Christ. He is fifty-one years old, married, and has four children. He graduated from the twelfth class of discipleship planters and represents the redemptive work of the Holy Spirit changing lives in India today. Here is his story:

My father partook in many worldly pleasures. He was a controlling master of our home and over my mother. My parents were not in unity, and I felt no peace around them. I was unable to get a formal education because my parents did not care for me. At a young age, I worried about how I was going to care for myself. I was naturally good at mechanics and learned how to fix motorbikes. Similar to my father, I associated with many bad people who were involved in crime. As a gang, we would rob and beat rich men. I even lost my teeth fighting people. I aimlessly traveled from place to place in India, causing trouble everywhere I went. I would drink until I fell intoxicated in the road. One day, my father told me to try praying to his god to make my life better. I went to one of the prominent temples with over two hundred thousand people.

When I got married, I continued my lifestyle of drinking and causing trouble. One day, I was on the roadside drunk and unconscious. When I came to and went home, my wife said, "I saw you with flies surrounding you on the roadside. Why do you do that?"

I began to think, "Why is my wife in the house and I am on the roadside? I go to the temple and worship, but this does not work. Is there truly a God?"

I made many temple sacrifices of fire, coconuts, chicken, and incense but did not understand why. I came to an understanding that there was no God, so I took the whole gang to the Communist party. Even the Hindus do not like Communists. Police would often chase after us, and it was normal for us to pay the police to release us. One day, a police officer pulled me over on my motorbike. I kicked him and quickly rode away. Then a gang of police officers came and severely beat me. I drank so much out of anger, and I wanted to kill them.

The gang of Communists and I would travel to hundreds of villages with a loudspeaker, yelling, "There is no god." I would stop prayer meetings and threaten Christians every chance I would get. I continued to drink six liters of alcohol a day and even steal alcohol.

A Christian man tried to show me love, but I was very cruel anytime he came near me. Once I was beaten so badly that I could not talk or move as I lay on the roadside. On the third day, the Christian man came to help me. He showed me much love and helped clean up my wounds. I still could not see well and could hardly talk. He began to share the gospel and love of Jesus. He told me that Jesus died for me and could heal my body. As he spoke these words, I heard him, but I could not see him because of the swelling in my face. When my eyesight came back to me, I saw that it was the Christian man who I had hated and mistreated.

Now I had a desire to show love back to this man. He continued to be kind and meet my daily needs. He cared for me, and God used him to heal my wounds. On the fourth day, I gave my life to Jesus. I traveled with this man to different places and shared my testimony. He was now my brother in Christ, my friend, and my family. He even took me to the area where I had promoted the Communist message of no god. As I shared my testimony in this area, the villagers knew me and believed my story. Many villagers came to Christ.

The Communist gang targeted me, harassed me, and tried to extort my money. As God continued to work in my life, one gang member gave his life to Christ. The Christian man started a weekly meeting at the ex-gang member's home. Many people who had committed adultery, stole, drank, and beat their wives gave their lives to Christ after hearing my testimony. I never knew Jesus could change the cold heart of man to a heart of flesh. Now I proclaim, "There is a God and his name is Jesus."

My story continued to spread to more and more people. Because I am not schooled, I prayed for many days to miraculously be able to read. I praise God because the Holy Spirit taught me how to read. God has become real to me through his Word. I have an increasing appetite to learn more about him every day. A year later, I met a discipleship planter in my village. I lived a long way away from a discipleship-planting school. It would take me three hours each way to get there, and I thought it was surely too far. But as I prayed, God told me he would help me with transportation and meet the need.

I joined the discipleship-planting school, and I thank God for the food, institution, and humble leaders. The real fellowship was a deep encouragement to me, and my whole family now knows the Lord. There were times when I had no money and would need to walk to school. Sometimes, I even missed a few classes. There was a time I was going to be late and a stranger walked up to me and gave me money for transportation to the school that day.

Please continue to pray for more villages to be reached with the love of Christ. God has put a predominantly Hindu village on my heart that is about fifty to sixty kilometers away. I don't have a motorbike but will use bus transportation. Thank you for your continued prayers and love.

***

I hope Sutish's story gives you great encouragement about God's power to transform very wicked people and then make them people who are productive members of their society. God changes people from violence and death to people of peace and life-givers. In the following chapter, we will hear what meetings look like when transformed people gather in hostile regions.

Chapter 10

Organic Church Meetings

The church is the people of God. Church meetings are where the disciples of God come together in intimate fellowship to build relationships. The Lord gave Pastor Singh simplicity in teaching four scriptural marks of a healthy church gathering. He calls them the four Ws: Welcome, Worship, Word, and Witness.

Welcome: It is of the utmost importance that each person who comes to a church meeting feels immediately welcome. In India, many who attend are poor and from the low caste, but the majority are from the demographic people group called *Dalits*, which means "untouchables" and is defined as "broken and scattered." This group numbers over 200 million in India. They are considered so unwanted and broken that they are not even given a caste ranking within Hinduism. As such, some people refer to them as "outcastes" (those who do not belong to a caste). For much of their life, they have not been welcomed in many circles. Expressing love to any guest is a powerful demonstration of the welcoming spirit of Christ. They begin each meeting by honoring and blessing the new guests. They practice hospitality and offer a seat, drink, and any food if available.

The Welcome is taught throughout Scripture. In the Old Testament, we see laws commanding care for foreigners, and the prophetic books order that we must welcome foreigners and strangers. *You shall treat the stranger who sojourns with you as the native among you, and you shall love him as yourself, for you were strangers in the land of Egypt: I am the LORD your God* (Leviticus 19:34 ESV).

Jesus taught us to welcome sinners and broken and hurting people. *Come unto me, all ye that labor and are heavily laden, and I will give you rest* (Matthew 11:28). Jesus also included women, children, old, and young, and even gentiles in his ministry. His original church was made up of many ethnic groups, degrees of power, and wealth – or the lack of it. We are to offer hospitality (Hebrews 13:2). We are to invite all to join Christ at the banquet table (Luke 14:21).

Worship: Ultimately, everything we do as disciples should be worthy acts unto the Lord. Meetings in India always have a concerted time of expressing to God that he is worthy. Worship, in its most basic form, is anything we choose to do or say to show that he is worthy of our affection and attention. Worship in India includes people giving a testimony, sharing a Bible verse, doing a dance, or singing praise. Most churches do not have the funds to buy musical instruments, nor have most believers had the opportunity to be trained. Drums are sometimes present, as making percussion instruments out of simple objects can be easy and inexpensive. Worship is not performance based but participation based because everyone is encouraged to make a joyful expression unto the Lord.

Word: The elders of each fellowship teach the Word. They teach passages of Scripture in a way that the congregation can learn the passage during the service and immediately share it with others. Many remote villages have high percentages of illiteracy. Therefore, passing out printed Bibles in these areas doesn't help. In India, there are over 2,400 tribal people groups, and most don't have Bibles translated into their languages yet. Since the village believers can learn stories and passages of Scripture at each meeting, they increase in their biblical knowledge.

The Indian leaders practice much inductive Bible study so they can teach and encourage the flock to listen and understand the Scriptures for themselves and then apply them in obedience. By teaching slowly like this, they give all of them tools and thus strengthen the priesthood of all believers to live by hearing and obeying God's Word. The natural next step is to then have the confidence to use God's Word to teach and train others.

Obedience to Scripture is foundational for the maturity of every believer. If God's Word says it, then it needs to be implemented. Therefore, praying for the sick, correcting ungodly behaviors, teaching in righteousness, and encouraging immediate repentance are all part of a gathering. In fact, if immediate trust in God's Word is not practiced at their time together – what good is it to ask the new believers to obey at home? Modeling godly behavior in welcoming, worship, word, and witness is a natural part of discipleship.

Biblically, there is no debate about whether or not Christians who are disciples of Jesus are to be rooted in God's Word. *All Scripture is breathed out by God and profitable for teaching, for reproof, for correction, and for training in righteousness* (2 Timothy 3:16 ESV).

Witness: A natural progression after teaching the Word of God is for the congregation to move into a time of witness. All the believers are encouraged to consider what family or neighbors might be blessed and encouraged by the teaching. The witness is the work of every believer to the community around them. The elders will never assign work for a witness. For instance, the pastor will not command some to go to the hospital, some to the school, some to go to the market, etc. The pastor will simply say, "Let's have a time of sharing how the Holy Spirit is leading us to witness to others."

The congregation will begin to share opportunities. One disciple might say, "My uncle is a Hindu and in the hospital sick. He is scared and asked me to come this Wednesday to pray for him."

Others in the group will often volunteer to join each other in ministry. The group will go for fifteen to twenty minutes as they tell about activities of serving and coordinating efforts to share the gospel with others.

All assemblies of believers practice the four Ws. In this way, the church continues to grow in an organic, simple form with quick reproduction. Discipleship is about doing life together. There are no set times to meet. Where love abounds, people delight in gathering together. In some villages, they meet daily. In others, they meet three times a week. Some are very restricted, and they must meet secretly at non-scheduled times as the Holy Spirit gives opportunity. The freedom of expression allows for much participation and focus on the needs of every community and those gathered.

Tulasi's Testimony of Leadership

My name is Tulasi, and I am a widow. I was raised in a strong Hindu home, and our belief system directed each aspect of our lives. Even our names are from different gods and goddesses. It goes back for several generations in my family. My name, Tulasi, comes from a significant and holy plant used in most homes to offer to gods as a morning prayer. My parents believed my name honored and pleased the gods, which made me the most lovable daughter of the gods. From my early childhood, my parents would offer many tulasi plant sacrifices in worship to many deities to get a lovely husband for me.

The time came, and I got married to a man who was very caring and loving for the first year. My health began to decline, and no gods, medications, or surgeries would help. Because of my sickness, I was unable to have a physical relationship with my husband. He began to beat and abuse me because I was unable to satisfy him sexually. One day, he left, and I didn't know where he went. I felt so lonely and broken because the only person I had ever loved was gone. My depression led to mental illness, and I had no control of my brain. I would run into the forest singing and talking like a madwoman. Gradually, I would take off my clothes and run around the village, scaring people. My parents were very ashamed of my life and desired for me to die.

A Christian brother came to our village, and my mom told him about me. To our surprise, the brother had heard about my situation. He shared with my mother that, at the edge of the village, a small group of Christians often met together for prayer for the sick. He asked if she would bring me to the home so they could pray over me for healing.

The next day, my family took me to the Christian home, and they all stood around me and prayed. The power of God touched me instantly, and I began to act normal. My angry demeanor, violent behavior, and disturbed spirit became quiet. Great joy came upon the faces of my parents. Rejoicing, we left the secret Christian home with an invitation to attend the Christian meetings a few times a week.

When we returned home, my parents were so upset with the Hindu gods and goddesses, and they asked why no god had cared about their daughter. We burned the holy plants, house temples, and other religious articles in our home. We stopped attending any Hindu gathering or activity. The very next week, my parents and I attended the Christian gathering and surrendered our lives to Jesus. The discipleship planter shared about the new kingdom and that this present world is temporary. He told us that by new birth we can enter into that new kingdom because we are born in the spirit and allow Christ to dwell in our hearts. He shared a Bible verse from John 3:3. *Truly, truly, I say to you, unless one is born again, he cannot see the kingdom of God* (ESV).

Since joining the Christian group, we have faced severe persecution in our village and from our relatives, but the Lord is keeping us safe. There is a mighty kingdom at work, and our small Christian group is growing stronger by the power of the Holy Spirit. The mighty Lord has moved my heart to serve people in surrounding villages and called me to be a kingdom worker. The discipleship planter confirmed this calling and connected me with the discipleship-planting schools. I joined the fifteenth class, and my passion for the lost increases greatly each day of my life.

***

Like Tulasi, let's pray that the passion for lost souls will increase in our lives as others become zealous for reaching our world for Christ. Tulasi's story also illustrates that all four Ws are a corporate experience. Specifically, the community of God's people served Tulasi and witnessed Christ in collaboration. Evangelism is not a lone-ranger activity and is most healthy in collaboration. Let's encourage obedience in each other to follow Christ all the days of our lives. The coming chapter will discuss the role of prayer and fasting in the growing revival movement in India.

Chapter 11

Prayer and Fasting

As I was writing this chapter, I just returned from India. Let me share with you what happened this past month. SOM–India inspired the global network of partners to participate in twenty-one days of prayer and fasting. Since ending the prayer and fasting, the Lord opened my eyes to see a buffet platter of answers. The twenty-one days ended two weeks before I was scheduled to fly to the next graduation. Leading up to our trip, the Indian network had been short on funds to cover the graduation expenses for nearly 600 students. The Lord orchestrated dramatic answered prayer, and the day after the prayer and fasting ended, the Lord provided all the funds needed for graduation. Not only had all the funds been met for graduation expenses but support for 120 bicycles for discipleship planters! Those provisions reflect the finances, not to mention the multiple spiritual blessings, that continue to be poured out upon us all. Prayer and fasting are foundational aspects of the work in India, and of any discipleship movement, because it is the heart of Christ. Please do not misunderstand that either the Indian believers or I would claim prayer and fasting is a formula to get God's favor and answered prayer; not at all! In fact, some prayer and fasting lasts for years, and God answers with a no. Ouch! This is not what we were hoping for.

Prayer is a relationship with God and a way to keep your heart tender and obedient. Jesus took much time to seek his Father in prayer. He taught us that after he ascended to his Father, his disciples should pray and fast. The Word of God tells us that the house of God will be a house of prayer for all people, not just the really righteous (Isaiah 56:7).

To appreciate healthy prayer in a movement of God, we need to recognize unhealthy prayer. Every religion has a prayer aspect as part of religious expression. What is the difference between religious babbling and genuine communication with the Creator, the God of the universe?

Jesus warned against practices of sinful prayer (Matthew 6:5). He taught us that our prayers should not be done to look good in front of others. We should not pray out of selfish gain to feed the flesh (James 4:3). We should not think that our many words gain God's favor (Matthew 6:7). We should not pray out of pride (Luke 18:10–14). We should not pray with unforgiveness (Mark 11:25). We should not lack faith (Matthew 21:22). We should not dishonor, nor be inattentive to our wives, lest it hinder our prayers (1 Peter 3:7). These are just a few warnings of how we should not pray.

Studies show that most people in the world pray. Specifically, I have noticed the deeply religious nature of Christians globally. Muslims pray five times a day. Devout Hindus start every morning with sacrifices made to their gods. In many regions of the world, I have found Christians praying for long periods of time, and even all night, with prayers and daily fasting, but their prayers are powerless. Why do I say this? As I have observed some of these networks of "religious Christians," I have been able to witness the fruit of flesh coming out of their lives. Their witness in the community is full of division, hatred, anger, envy, sexual immorality, jealousy, and the like. We will know a tree by its fruit (Matthew 7:20). The outcome of praying Christians does not automatically equate to fruit-bearing Christians. If a Christian community is not seeing the multiplication of God's glory and maturity in Christ, then the discipleship womb is sterile.

Powerful prayers bring transformation from lives of depravity to lives of holiness and obedience. Powerless prayer doesn't change anything. Powerless prayer just makes the flesh look more religious. Fasting doesn't make one holy. It can have the effect of making one angrier as he becomes hungrier. If Christianity religiously feeds the flesh, it must be managed by fleshly means. This is not a healthy situation, and unfortunately, there are many fleshly prayer services held around the world.

So, what does healthy prayer look like when it comes out of a movement of the Holy Spirit? Jesus had much to say and do about genuine prayer, and I encourage everyone to do a study on the prayers of Jesus. Concisely, powerful prayer comes from a clean heart that is desperate to experience God's love. It's a relationship with God. Like any relationship, it's a two-way experience of listening, obeying, and communicating our thoughts, feelings, and questions.

It's transparent communication with God. God loves humble, authentic, broken, transparent communication with him. God is real and responds well to unadulterated prayer (i.e., "God help me!").

Love is the motivation for God to hear from us. Effective prayer from his people comes from a heart of love. Love covers over a multitude of bad prayers (1 Peter 4:7–8). In summary, healthy prayer is not a religious expression but a living, growing relationship.

The following story depicts a discipleship planter and his place of prayer.

Boriah's Testimony of Leadership

My name is Boriah. I was born into a Hindu tribal family and am now married. I was miraculously healed from jaundice, which caused me to respond in faith to Jesus and I was spiritually saved in 1992. In 2009, I was called to the ministry, and I began to share the gospel and my testimony.

As people came to know the Lord, I discerned in my spirit the need for them to be equipped with the Word of God and directed in their daily lives. I myself didn't know the Word very well as I had not had the opportunity to learn more. I was deeply inspired when I heard of Pastor Singh's vision for discipleship-planting schools that was about to be launched. There was a group of committed people praying and seeking God for instruction and to equip people for effective ministry. In 2011, they launched the first school, and I was one of the students.

When I enrolled in the training, leaders groomed me in the Word, and I became more passionate about ministry. I practiced what I learned in my home village and began witnessing for Christ. I gathered people in my home as we learned together, and I instructed others to witness. I saw God moving in each of the home meetings in a huge way. Though there was no pulpit, no soundbox, no music, and no traditional church setup, the movement of God was very real. People would be lying on the mud floor and weeping for hours for the lost and dying. Many received a deep passion for the lost. As I graduated and was commissioned, my people were more excited for me to instruct them in the Word of God.

As one house group fasted and prayed for more laborers, the Lord began to stir the hearts of many people. The Lord raised up twenty-seven discipleship planters from the surrounding villages. After I instructed them on the basics, I enrolled them in the discipleship-planting school. They became equipped with the Word of God, and they serve with me in various villages. Praise God for the discipleship-planting movement and USA partners who invested their lives and resources to equip a person like me to multiply the kingdom work in India. We have a total of 137 fellowships planted under my leadership, and we are still working hard for more churches.

Praise God for the tools such as Bibles, the DVDs of *God's Story* and *Jesus Film*, bicycles, and Shepherd's Staff (pastor's manual). We thank God for the partnership of World Missionary Assistance Plan, or better known as World MAP, who donated Shepherd's Staff manuals for all discipleship planters, which is currently just under five thousand!

These tools were provided for me and the discipleship planters in my area to reach the villages effectively. We thank the Lord each day for our USA and India partners who stand with us in prayer and encouragement, building the kingdom of God in the Hindu villages of India.

I am diabetic, and my wife is barren. She suffers from thyroid issues. My wife and I felt the urgency to give all our time to the Lord's work. We live by faith, and God provides miraculously by the village laborers who are part of the house groups. Though our daily provisions are met, it's hard for us to get medical care, but Jesus has been our only medicine. Please pray for my family and the discipleship-planting network in our area.

***

As we think about prayer in our lives and ministry today, I encourage you to ask the Lord to evaluate your prayer life. Ask the Lord what he wants to change. Have a conversation with God about how you can grow in prayer and encouragement to others; pray for his kingdom to come and his will to be done on earth as in heaven. In the next chapter, we will see how our prayer turns into practical help.

Chapter 12

Practical Help: Lighthouse Sewing Centers

When I first met Pastor Singh, he gave me one piece of advice: practical theology is everything Indians need. They need to immediately understand God's Word and then apply it. He said, "There are some Indian teachers who are brilliant. They teach deep doctrines, and some educated Indians will understand them. Yet, by the time the masses of Indians understand what the educated Christians are teaching, millions of Indians will be dead and in a Christless eternity." There is a beauty to faith when it is daily lived in meeting the spiritual, emotional, and physical needs of others.

One of the first pressing needs discovered in the beginning days of this work was that of the widows. Some husbands were divorcing women who came to Christ. These women had no skill, were rejected by their village, and they were shunned for their faith and isolated from getting help from others. Most widows in the network have little education and cannot read.

The Word of God promises that the Lord hears the prayers of the widows and is a husband to them. Certainly, the work in India has highlighted God's attentive care for widows. In 2012, the first Lighthouse women's sewing and discipleship school was started with four ladies. The schools are held alongside discipleship-planting schools to nurture relationships with more mature Christians who are available to assist in travel to and from schools. These schools keep the same schedule of six months and participate in graduation ceremonies with the discipleship planters.

The schools are staffed by an instructor who volunteers time to train in the skills of sewing garments. With a bare-bones budget, they use newspapers to learn how to cut patterns on fabric. Each school has two sewing machines to train ten women. The sewing machines are manual, foot-pedal powered. These machines are an advantage for us as they are cheaper to buy and maintain, and they don't depend upon electricity, which can be sporadic in many of the poor villages. We make no promises that they will receive a sewing machine upon completion of training. They must trust the Lord and ask for his provision. Thus far, we have been able to train and provide at graduation a one-hundred-dollar sewing machine for over 1,800 women at the time of this writing.

It takes us an average of thirty hours of travel from the USA to visit India every six months for the graduations. The joyous, bright smiles of these women are a great part of our reward.

Pastor Singh is consistent in communicating that all social help is always for one thing: to proclaim the gospel of Jesus Christ so that we make more disciples for him. Whenever he speaks of the Lighthouse sewing centers, he is quick to mention how these sewing centers are not really about the economics of these women having a way to provide for their family. Nor is it about the social elevation of these women. It is about equipping each to be a light in the dark villages and share Christ with others.

During my most recent trip to India, I visited a Lighthouse center. Mahima had graduated six months before in the sixteenth class. When we arrived, over fifty Indians greeted us with huge smiles and showered us with flower petals. The bright, colorful saris, smiles, aroma of flowers, and joyful greetings were like a symphony of love, and consequently, the SOM team felt very welcomed. If that was not enough to make us feel honored, the Indian leadership washed our feet with milk and rinsed them with water. We were all humbled beyond words and experienced the maturity of Christ in his church. These people truly loved us.

Even more inspiring was Mahima's story. She came from a Hindu background of brokenness, pain, and suffering. Her husband had abandoned her. She was destitute until some Indians shared the love of Christ with her. While growing in Christ, she heard about the Lighthouse training and joined the sixteenth class. I asked her how many people she had prayed with in the past six months. About 1,200 ladies, she told me.

We asked her again, "Maybe you misunderstood us. How many people each month have you prayed for."

She answered, "Yes, I have been blessed to pray for about 200 ladies each month."

We were awestruck! In addition, we learned that a couple of dozen ladies regularly meet at her home for worship and God's Word.

Mahima represents over 1,800 ladies, and growing, that have been changed from powerlessness into leaders of transformation. Through the years, the network has reached out by providing cleaning projects, disaster relief, food, clothing, transportation, and more in times of dire need. One thing is always connected to humanitarian relief, and that is the proclamation of the gospel of Jesus Christ. As Pastor Singh would say, how can we love people and hold back our greatest gift of people knowing Jesus?

Malla's Testimony of Leadership

My name is Malla. I gave my life to the Lord one year ago at a Christian gathering in North India. My husband passed away two years ago and left a huge debt of three thousand US dollars. I was alone and living in a small house as I faced many struggles with the moneylender. The lender would call me to the village elder meetings, where I would be judged on my debt and abused with vulgar words. The lender threatened to take my small home. The pressure of the debt pushed me to seek many gods and goddesses for help.

I contemplated suicide because I would then be set free from the debt. While battling this irrational thought, someone invited me to a Christian home for food and fellowship. I had no idea what they did but thought I could at least talk to some people since others in my village overlooked me for being a widow with debt. When I entered the home, the people were very loving and filled with hopeful conversations. I heard about God's love and how Christ demonstrated that love by suffering. It broke my heart yet filled my empty heart with greater joy. Immediately, a tear rolled down my cheek, and I felt deep repentance for not knowing Jesus. I gave my life to Jesus that day. I began to grow in love and in my prayer life.

For some time, I hid the fact that I was a Christian, but eventually, my neighbors realized I was praying with Christians in other villages. These neighbors would speak evil over me and give me much trouble for my faith. When the moneylender heard about my newfound faith, he was furious. He told me I could no longer stay in my home. He said, "I am calling the police, locking up your home, and selling it. You do not deserve to live here any longer."

I tried to request a few more days to give me time to find another place to live, but the lender didn't allow it. I began to pray and left the village with only the clothes on my back. The Christian family in the other village welcomed me warmly. They prayed with me, and it brought me great encouragement.

The Christian family shared about the Lighthouse training and some of the ladies' testimonies. This was a great opportunity from the Lord. I enrolled in the training and graduated with the ninth class. I was empowered with God's Word and skill to meet the needs of others. The Lord blessed me with a brand-new sewing machine. I began my Lighthouse trade in a tiny house provided by the Christian family. The Lord continues to draw customers to my home. He meets my daily needs and equips me to serve many women, children, and broken people in my village.

Please pray for continued boldness and response for the kingdom of God.

***

The Lighthouse women continue to make an impact for Christ in the lost villages of India. Sometimes these women are misunderstood and face persecution from the villagers. Some Hindus spread lies and slander the Lighthouse ladies, saying they are paid to be in the village not just for the trade but to convert people to Christ. The reality is that Lighthouse sewing ladies and discipleship planters are never paid. They live by faith and apply their skills for loving others. These women crave your prayers for continued boldness and to be a light in these spiritually dark villages.

There is a need for practical support in the exploding Indian network of believers. It's all connected to the Word of God and transforming the church into people of righteousness, grace, and truth. These transformed people are transforming others with simple tools that meet the needs and communicate love.

Chapter 13

Serving

Christ came not to be served, but to serve (Matthew 20:28). One of the attributes we have observed through my past nine years working in India among the discipleship-planting movement is the maturity of serving one another. India is a culture of honor and shame and power and fear. Specifically, people obey those in authority without question and serve them with respect.

The Lord raised up Pastor Singh to launch a mighty discipleship movement that presently averages twenty congregations planted daily. For each graduation, he invites delegates from the SOM International network to attend to honor and inspire the graduates. During this ceremony, he honors others, and when the time comes for the distribution of diplomas, he often sits in the audience and lets other Indian leaders and the international delegation congratulate the graduates as they cross the stage. He is in a constant state of serving and deferring honor to others.

You can tell much about a man from his family. During our visits, we are able to spend much time with Pastor Singh's wife and his two sons. Singh's wife is an amazing cook. With joy, she is quick to offer us fruits and milk chai. Her meals are scrumptious. The serving DNA is also clearly manifested upon his two young sons. They are consistently quiet and listen with active observation. Often, they will fetch tissue paper, a pen and paper, a bottle of water, or a pillow before the request is even made as they anticipate needs. Whenever we exit a vehicle, the Indian Christian workers immediately show up to take our bags. The integrity of their service is not just targeted to foreigners. Regularly, we have observed the Singh family giving gifts to needy people, praying for the hurting, and feeding the hungry.

When we attend meetings, we must often guess who the top leaders are as everyone helps set up. If there is any competition among these Indian Christians, it is to out-serve one another. During a recent visit, the leadership conference was planned for three hundred attendees, which was the maximum occupancy. When the building became swarmed with over four hundred Indians and more coming, Pastor Singh made a call to the owner of a conference hall twice the size one block down the road. The building was available. Everyone grabbed chairs, musical equipment, food, and cooking utensils, etc. In unity, we made the transition to the bigger building. I was amazed to witness the move completed and our meeting resumed in twenty minutes. This test was a clear demonstration that this movement is a group of activists who all want to be a part of the action and are willing to get their hands dirty.

The way the leadership models serving is contagious. We have visited dozens of remote and rural villages, and the new believers are quick to help. They share their food and buy us bottled water and soda pop. They often want to present tokens of love to us, such as handcrafted household goods. We have even been given Indian rupees (money) as a contribution to continue the work, which, considering their worldly poverty, are mighty gifts equivalent to the widow's mite.

One of the aspects that empowers the village congregations is the credibility of their serving. Many villagers, who viewed Christians as a threat to other religious ways of life, have been won over by the consistent labor of love and unity among the believers. The following is a story that illustrates the growing influence of the gospel in India by acts of service among remote villages.

Remote Village Congregation Testimony of Leadership

Some of our discipleship planters started a Christian fellowship in a strong, fanatic Hindu community. Their lives shined the light of Christ so brightly that they began to reach out and reflect their light to the surrounding villages. They were very touched and agonized by the deep spiritual darkness in these Hindu villages.

They were so hungry for the Lord and to reach the lost that they would meet for fellowship, Bible study, and intercessory prayers four to five times a week. In less than twelve months, they planted nineteen congregations, and they rejoiced, but their hearts continued to break for a Hindu school in the area. The school had been there for more than two decades, and there was no Christian work in the school at all.

The children were taught Hindu prayers and words from Hindu books at the beginning and end of their classes. The teachers and other staff were mainly Hindus and a few Muslims.

The children in the school were quite mischievous and misbehaved when they had free time. The home fellowship members were filled with compassion when they saw the behavior of hundreds of children in that school. They felt pity for the children because they were helpless and didn't know better. The discipleship planters walked around in the school area praying against everything that locked the students into darkness.

Several times, they tried to share the gospel and gain access in the school for ministry, but there was no way because it was tightly locked with Hinduism. They prayed for doors to be opened. As they prayed, the Lord gave them an idea to go and ask permission to clean the school premises and surroundings, which were filthy.

With permission granted, they cut the plants, leveled the roads, burned the weeds, and cleaned the premises. After cleaning, one Christian walked into the school office to inform the principal they were done and said they would love to pray with him if there are any problems or issues in the school.

The principal asked, "What is prayer?"

The worker said, "Seeking help from our God."

He was silent for a while, then walked out of his office to see the cleaned area. The principal was amazed because it was so meticulously cleaned and looked great.

The principal was very grateful, and he was now interested in spending time with the Christians; he invited them to join him for coffee and tea. They had a good feeling to ask him if they could spend time with the kids and teach them different games, dances, and moral stories. The principal gave them the opportunity.

With much joy, they began to play with the children and sing, dance, and tell Bible stories. They told fifteen stories in the school in three weeks. The most impactful story was of baby Moses, especially the divine hand behind his adoption and Egyptian education and how the Lord called him and used him as a leader. The children in the school were 90 percent of Hindu background and a few of Islamic background and other non-Christian faiths.

More than three hundred children were part of the after-school ministries, and eighty-five children truly opened their hearts and gave their lives to Jesus! Praise God. They scattered into small groups and had fellowship, song time, Bible stories, and prayer. Please pray for their growth and witness.

Getting together in big groups frequently will get the attention of the public, and it will cause trouble for the school staff. So, the discipleship planters avoid big gatherings. Some children are learning how to work with others in the school. Also, there are some people who have suspicious eyes on the activities, and if anyone reports it to the government, the staff will be at risk, including the principal. Praise God that he is using the school staff as men of peace and pray that they will know Jesus personally in their lives.

***

That is one example of how the discipleship planters look for any type of opportunity to reach out and bring people to the Lord. With prayer and obedience, any tiny thing in our lives can bring someone to the Lord. The Christian fellowships that they plant are reproducing and multiplying. As someone said, "Raising the dead can be hard, but giving birth is easy." Now there are over five thousand discipleship planters who strive to reach the Hindu, Muslim, Buddhist, cultural Christian, and animistic tribal villages for Christ.

In the next chapter, we will examine how persecution and Jesus's martyr spirit unites and inspires the Indian and global network.

Chapter 14

The Spirit of Martyrdom

At the writing of this book, India is tenth on the list of the most persecuted nations according to Open Doors' annual World Watch List. Pastor Singh and his wife have been physically attacked for their faith. They teach their leaders to expect persecution, and they explain how persecution is part of God's way of refining the community of God's people.

On my first visit with Pastor Singh in 2012, I was able to spend two days with thirty of his top leaders. During that time, I told them many stories of persecution against Christians around the world, and I encouraged their faith with truth from the Word of God. At the end of that time, many of the leaders requested that they receive regular updates on their persecuted global family. They had never heard these reports because the media in India does not share stories about the persecution of Christians. They shared their desire to pray for the suffering body of Christ, and these testimonies of faith have helped them persevere.

Within the year, SOM–India was born, and Pastor Singh and his wife began a monthly newsletter with national and global updates to encourage God's people.

The monthly distribution of newsletters, which are shared by hand, now exceeds forty thousand.

In John 10, which tells the story of the good shepherd, Jesus illustrates the difference between a mature disciple and a disciple of the flesh. The "hired hand" is the shepherd who tends God's people (the sheep), but when suffering comes (a wolf), the immature disciple will run from his job because his desire is to protect his flesh and his personal livelihood over protecting God's people. In contrast, the mature man of God (good shepherd) is willing to suffer and even die for God's people and his work. Thus, the awakening in India is producing good shepherds with a spirit of martyrdom due to their faith. They are willing to obey God's voice even to the detriment of their own flesh.

The global directors of SOM International all have a martyr's spirit. This confidence is multiplied as a spiritual inheritance for everyone who joins the work. Our direction is straight from the Lord. God's mature children only have one pastor, and that is Pastor Jesus. As we cleanly represent the character of Christ, we are his assistant pastors/shepherds in this world. The sheep will only recognize his voice and direction.

The name of our ministry sounds strange to most people. Even more so when confessing to others that we have a spirit of martyrdom. The flesh of man does not want to die to its own will. The Scripture is clear that death to the old man is necessary in order to qualify to receive a martyr's crown and the robe of righteousness that are the reward from the heavenly Father. The will of humankind must surrender completely to the will of God.

The word for martyr in Scripture comes from the Greek word *martus*, which is used thirty-four times in the New Testament Greek Received Text manuscript. Most of the time it is translated as "witness." A clean witness is one who will not compromise their testimony even in the face of persecution. More often, in the New Testament, those called martyrs (martus) are living witnesses, not yet having the testimony of a martyr's death.

Consider the list of those named as martyrs (martus) in the Word of God: God is a martyr (1 Thessalonians 2:5); Jesus is a martyr (Revelation 1:5); Holy Spirit is a martyr (Acts 5:32); martyrs are the disciples still living during the church age (Acts 2:32); the apostle John, who was the one apostle not to die a violent death (Acts 1:22); Stephen (Acts 22:20); all those who faithfully lived for God during the Old Testament age (Hebrews 12:1); and anyone who was a credible witness (Matthew 18:16).

I believe God has richly blessed SOM–India and the entire SOM Global Network for this very spirit of martyrdom. This spirit produces the work of God that flows from a clean heart of martyrdom. For the Lord to make a spotless and blameless bride for Christ, he raises up martyrs to lead the body of Christ courageously. God will make his witness clean!

I was honored to commission Kumar as a discipleship planter at one of our graduations. Kumar convinced his brother to join in the work. Together they traveled long journeys to preach the gospel in restricted villages. Kumar's brother was killed for his Christian leadership a few months later. The Lord has greatly used the example of these workers and inspired many other Indian leaders.

Kumar's Testimony of Leadership

My name is Kumar, and I was born in a remote village of North India. I was a fanatical, zealous Hindu who worshiped everything except Christ. I believed in the millions of gods and goddesses. The priest of our village would demand our loyalty. During certain seasons, he would offer sacrifices and tell us that harm and danger were awaiting us if we didn't give him a lot of money.

One day, something strange began to happen in my father's life. He lost his temper and acted out aggressively. He would sometimes run away from the family for weeks to live in the jungles and sleep in burial grounds. Many times, we had to go out to the jungle, tie him up, and bring him home. He would not eat any food or drink any water for weeks. The priest of the village said one of the powerful deities was not happy with him and had descended on his body to destroy him. We needed to appease the deity with rituals. We believed the priest and paid him our very last coin, and my father's mind did not change at all.

One day, a discipleship planter visited our village and prayed for my father and then left. Instantly, my father began to act normal, eat food, and drink water; he never ran away from home again. It was a miracle, and we invited the discipleship planter to come back. He shared about the true living God, Jesus.

The whole family accepted Jesus as their Savior. The villagers rejected us and threatened us with death if we continued to proclaim the name of Jesus.

I experienced great joy and felt a heavy burden to share this truth. My hunger to hear from God and learn the Word grew each day. I got connected with the discipleship-planting schools and enrolled in the eleventh class. The day I enrolled, I began to seek the face of the Lord by fasting and praying about where God was going to lead me to minister. Before my training ended, the Lord spoke to me the name of a village far away. I had no idea how I would get there, and I fasted in prayer again.

The day after graduation, I felt the Lord telling me to walk to the remote village. It was a three- to four-hour walk each way. I drank the creek water on the side of the road to hydrate myself as I walked. When I arrived at the village, it was spiritually dark and hard to share the gospel, but the Lord began to stir in my heart that this was the village where he would show his glory.

"Don't fear; witness my power." The Lord began to move and penetrate the hearts of the Hindu villagers, and four families came to the Lord on that first visit. One woman saw the vision of Jesus hanging on the cross and wept for hours.

A villager opened their home and I began to visit the village once a week to pray and teach the Word of God. The main Indian fanatical Hindu group, the Rashtriya Swayamsevak Sangh (RSS), observed the ministry and threatened to kill me many times. The Lord put such a deep love in my heart for the people that I continued to visit. A few months had passed, and a small group of believers from my village joined me on my walk, including my younger brother. That night when we returned to my village, it was so dark we could not see anyone on the road. Three RSS members rode up behind us at high speed on a motorbike; they ran over my brother and injured two other women. In minutes, my brother was sinking in a pool of blood and gave his last breath before being with Jesus for eternity.

The next day, my parents and I walked to the spot where my brother was killed and stood with heaviness in our heart, but also with deep praise to our God. Though nobody stood with us at that time, we felt the presence of Jesus standing with us.

The police came to the spot and shouted, "Why have you brought a new religion to the village and faced such trouble?"

The local newspaper reported only an accident of a Christian. The villagers did not allow us to bury my brother in the village because he was a Christian, so my parents and I took his body to the far outskirts of the village. The RSS and villagers threatened that no other Christian should join us for the burial, or they would be killed.

One discipleship-planting leader asked how they could be praying for me, and I responded, "Please pray for us to be more effective in serving the Lord and be empowered by the Holy Spirit. Also, pray for the RSS biker who killed my brother to become a discipleship planter."

I'm praying for the surrounding villages to have Christian witnesses and hear the story of my brother who was martyred for Christ. In my discipleship-planting training, I learned that the blood of the martyr is the seed of the church. I pray that will literally happen in my region.

My parents and I are strengthened in our faith by my brother's life. The threats continue from the RSS, saying that they meant to run over me and not my brother. The discipleship-planting leaders in my area are a continual encouragement to me. Recently, I was given a brand-new bicycle as a great tool to plant more Christian fellowships in the surrounding villages. I'm so thankful to the assistance of the SOM-USA family for helping me be equipped and covering me in prayer as I continue to reach lost souls for Christ in India.

***

Kumar's example shows that the spirit of martyrdom is a mark of leadership. It is a compulsion to love God and others radically. What others often miss is that a spirit of martyrdom is also a spirit of life, joy, and true freedom.

In the last chapter, we want to demonstrate how this explosion of the gospel in India connects to the latter days of God's redemptive history. We also will show how the Lord is using this movement to spark a global awakening.

Chapter 15

Global End Times?

At the time I'm writing this book, within the SOM–India network, 683 home fellowships were planted in the month of June 2020 (during the COVID-19 pandemic). That calculates to an average of twenty-three churches planted each day, with an average of 460 Indians being saved daily in the network. These fruits do not count other good works happening in India that we're mostly unaware of. India is experiencing a revival among the remote, unreached, and low caste of society.

Are all these reports signs of the end times? We can confidently say yes! The Word of God points toward the time of Jesus as the beginning of the end times and the fulfillment of God's redemptive story. Jesus also prophetically tells us, *And this gospel of the kingdom shall be preached in all the world for a witness unto all nations, and then shall the end come* (Matthew 24:14).

The Greek word here for "nations" is translated from *ethnos*. Ethnos includes all people groups. The Joshua Project reports that 40 percent of the world is still unreached. It also points out that less than 3 percent of all Christian resources are used to bring the gospel to the least-reached and the most persecuted 40 percent. SOM International is honored to be a conduit of invested resources, and we have a great passion for recruiting more of the body of Christ to pour resources into the neediest 40 percent of the world's people. We see not only the greatest need in these unreached and restricted regions but also the best opportunities. The Holy Spirit is currently working in dramatic ways to reach these underserved and unreached three billion people.

India is not alone in exponential growth among people groups. The SOM Global Network reports other revivals and encouraging signs of increase. During the past few months that the world has endured the pandemic of COVID-19, SOM–Bangladesh reported eighteen home fellowship plants, and ninety-seven Bangladeshis were baptized.

Northwest Africa just graduated 210 mostly Muslim-background discipleship planters. They report daily of Muslims coming to Christ from many different tribes. They are planting home fellowships in unreached villages. SOM–Senegal Director Saidou said, "When I first came to Christ in 1998, I could name to you all the ex-Muslim believers on both hands. By 2012, I could name every ex-Muslim in our country and in what village they live. Now, I cannot name all the believers even in one village. The Lord is on the move."

SOM–South America Director Russell currently sends me weekly updates regarding the exploding revival in Venezuela. Economic and social chaos has devastated Venezuela, and an estimated four million Venezuelans have left the country and are now living as refugees. Venezuela's past economic livelihood was from gas exportation. When petroleum was over one hundred dollars a barrel, Venezuelans were basking in abundance. Those days are over, and now the current pandemic has made a bad situation only worse. The average Venezuelan wage is down to five to ten dollars per month. They struggle for daily shelter and food.

We have discovered that the Venezuelan socialist government did not promote Bible production or distribution of any kind during the past two decades. In the past year, we found some churches where the pastor did not even have a Bible and other congregations that only had one Bible. The majority of Venezuelan Christians do not own a personal Bible. Very few Christians have received a new Bible during the past twenty years, and access to new Bibles has practically been non-existent. As we have moved through Venezuela, we have seen football-field-length lines of people queued to receive a new Bible. Even more surprising is the receptivity we have received from the military, police, and government officials. All of them have begged us for more Bibles and requested that their personnel receive one. Many of the distributions have included military and police oversight in the distribution. Schools, businesses, hospitals, and jails have requested Bible distributions.

I recently visited this area along the Colombia/ Venezuela border. I have personally never heard such desperate stories of people wanting the Bible. The Venezuelans dress up in their best clothes when receiving their Bible. Some citizens have traveled seven hours to get one. As one lady received her Bible, she shared through tears that she dreamed the night before that God would send his Word. The next morning, the Bible distribution team visited her town. Another man belonged to a Communist militia group along the border. He dreamed that God would change his life, bless Venezuela, and bring him and his buddy a Bible. The next morning, his whole platoon was killed in a shootout except for him and his friend. Soon after this, he met the Bible distribution team and received his Bible.

A Venezuelan police officer shared this story: "God has shown me that the situation will get much worse before it gets better. This crisis is necessary to remove corruption and cleanse the country down to its very foundation. At the same time, I have been shown that God will once again bless our nation, beginning with widespread distribution of the Bible."

During his years of serving Latin America, Russell observed that much of the spread of cults and religious contamination resulted from poor Spanish Bible translations. The Lord led Russell to edit an updated Spanish version of the Bible to reflect the meaning from the original Hebrew and Greek languages. He completed this project from 1990 to 2000. In English, we call this Spanish version the Jubilee Bible. Denominational leaders in Venezuela have been receiving this Spanish translation with joy. Upon review, they report back to us how encouraged they are, and for many, this is their new favorite translation. We observe a spirit of unity and love not seen in the past. Recently, one of the pastors was able to give President Maduro a copy of the Jubilee Bible while on live television. President Madura praised the gift and proclaimed that it would be read to his family and placed in his living room.

From 2019–2020, SOM–South America printed and distributed over 170,000 Bibles and New Testaments into Venezuela. We have also distributed many other Christian materials. We are praying for the Lord to raise resources to print and distribute over two million Bibles soon into Venezuela. I invite you to go to **biblesforvenezuela.com** for more details.

SOM International is also assisting leadership in Bangladesh, China, Colombia, Cuba, Gambia, Guinea-Bissau, Guinea-Conakry, Mali, Mauritania, and Mexico. Each of these nations has encouraging stories of God's work and workers.

As we began this book, I pointed out that India is the least-reached nation on earth, with 2,276 unreached people groups and 1.3 billion people. This unreached list does not include the countries of Pakistan, Bangladesh, and Nepal, which only magnifies the gaping spiritual darkness of the Indian subcontinent. That the Lord is giving so much attention to this lost region is exciting and points toward the latter days.

We also can say that all this is the end times because every one of us will die. In the spectrum of world history, let alone eternity, our death will be very soon. Therefore, one of the results from reviewing this book is, hopefully, to produce a godly sense of expectancy and urgency upon every Christian. These are the days that we need to filter the worldly broadcast news and focus on God's news. We need to see what the Lord is doing and join him. The Scriptures remind us that only what is prayed, done, and given in Christ's name will last (i.e., in unity with Christ and his glory). What we do from this moment forward is our eternal legacy.

I hope this book may spur every reader to recognize what the Lord is doing locally, nationally, and globally and consider how to get involved. We have documented the accounts of Indian believers and then shown their biblical patterns to inspire you to order your life, influence, and ministry according to God's ways. In God's kingdom, he is the authority, and his Word orders our life. Remember, the Lord's prayer is, *your will be done on earth, as it is in heaven* (Matthew 6:10 ESV).

Humankind cannot produce a revival or church-planting movement. Only the Holy Spirit can bring this kind of fruit. What we can do is obey God's Word and pattern our lives and congregations after his Word. Historically, when people humble themselves and seek God's will, it prepares the soil of hearts for revival and God's favor.

Practically, I encourage you to review this book a chapter at a time with other leaders. Take each discipleship principle and the stories to heart. Let each chapter encourage deep biblical thought and meditation on God's Word.

If this book has touched you, please sign up for the Spirit of Martyrdom International updates. We always look to expand our relationships with kingdom-minded Christians. Feel free to email us any testimonies or thoughts you have to contribute. Consider getting more copies of this book to give to others. Pray about what a discipleship-planting movement would look like in the United States or your home country. If SOM International can help you move in obedience, let us know. Keep in mind how God uses the faithfulness of little people to do his grand work.

In chapter 9, we told the story of Sutish, who was blinded for the first few days from recognizing the identity of the Indian good Samaritan. Finally, his eyes were opened, and Sutish recognized the Indian man as the one he had persecuted. After his eyes and heart were opened, Sutish began to help others. Is this a metaphor for the church? Today, are we the blind being awakened by the miraculous testimonies of the Indian church? Or are we the good Samaritan finding the blind Indian unreached soul on our path?

Either way, over one billion people in India are currently blind and deaf to the gospel. Together, we can assist them by spreading the light. If this book has touched your heart, we want to hear from you. If you want to share this book with others, contact us about bulk distribution or for ways we can collaborate for the greater glory of God. We invite you to view our store on our website, where you will find many other like-minded books and resources.

Endorsements Addendum

An amazing book that shows the Spirit of the Lord moving and working in the hearts of the discarded people of India. Our new brothers and sisters are not only responding in faith but in action. Their testimonies of rejection, salvation, and persecution swell with faith and love as Jesus meets them in their need. I was deeply moved and found that I was connected to the believers in India. This book is a beautiful call to join them and to tell people about the person and salvation of Jesus Christ.

—Bill Hickey, *retired public high school teacher*

The testimonies in this book are motivating. The people of India become bold witnesses right when they are converted. They know the cost. They have counted it and still courageously witness. The reading of this book will inspire you to be a bolder witness for the Lord Jesus Christ.

—Corey Smith, *child of the living God*

Awakening in India is a challenging and inspiring read. The personal stories of the faith and perseverance of our brothers and sisters in India will encourage and inspire you as they face an increasingly hostile culture but remain faithful to God's calling. One of the things that impressed me most was the testimonies of the power of the gospel to change lives. Their unsurpassed joy of having Christ over anything else in this world. How much we need to rediscover that joy in the church in our culture, and what a difference we could make if we did.

It also shows God's faithfulness in the midst of persecution and suffering. I'd highly encourage this book to all who have a heart for our persecuted brothers and sisters and find strength and encouragement through their stories as they share in the sufferings of Christ.

—David and Kim Reed, The Voice of The Martyrs voice representatives

David Witt initiated and continues to administer one of the most effective and efficient Christian outreaches active in our world. Through it, he and an exceptionally small and committed staff deeply improve thousands of lives spiritually and physically on a global basis, with unique specializations in Latin America, the Indian subcontinent, and Northwest Africa. David's story is one of proven character and results. He is finishing well.

—Doug Feavel, Christian author

David Witt takes us behind the scenes to a church-planting movement in India that is reshaping that nation. As churches are planted, lives are being supernaturally transformed, the sick are healed, and families reunited.

Pastor Singh sparked the movement in modeling a passion for spreading the good news in his native country. He is like the apostle Paul in the early Christian church.

The emerging church in India is not without persecution because of Hindu strongholds, which continue to bind and darken the hearts of the people. As a result, David Witt and Spirit of Martyrdom International have committed their considerable influence and resources to support Pastor Singh, train church planters, and meet the practical needs of those in the movement. In that all-important supporting role, Pastor Witt is witness to the stories, drama, and changed lives about which he writes.

This book brings enormous encouragement, hope, and evidence that God, through his Holy Spirit, is alive and moving in ways that few would have anticipated.

—Doug Fitzpatrick, *Attorney at Law*

God's leading has enabled David Witt in Awakening in India to open eyes and hearts to the wonderful way God works in bringing his truth to the world. The premise: a big God, using unnoticed, "little" people to change a world that even powerful governments cannot subdue. The principle of multiplying evangelism by using simple methods that rely on God's direction, not man's programs, while using only the Bible as a text, provides ways to evangelize and then support fellow believers in spiritually oppressed nations. Welcoming souls to worship and learn the Word progresses to their witness. Best of all, this is shared with true-life testimonies that will grip your heart forever. Throughout years of medical evangelism in dozens of countries, I have looked into the eyes of thousands of these spiritually hungry souls, wondering what story God will have for them to tell about how he reached them. A quick read with a life-long impact!

—Dr. Buck McNeil, Medical Doctor

The time is short; the end-time harvest is ready! But how do we bring it in? David Witt lays out this uncompromised mission of the church and the simple biblical pattern to fulfill it. The methods are practical, effective, and applicable in any culture or nation – just as Jesus, the Lord of the church, intended. Using real-life testimonies to show the divine power in "knowing Christ and making him known," this volume of anointed wisdom is a must-read for every believer in every nation!

—Dr. Frank Parrish, President of World MAP

I have always admired David's walk with Christ. He exhibits extraordinary faith in his daily walk as he serves those who risk much for Jesus, risking much himself. David takes this same passion and pours it into this book, placing readers on a journey into the latter days with a focus on India. The timing of his book with world events and alignment with Scripture, specifically in Matthew 24, where Jesus provided six signs that help us identify and prepare for the end times is thought-provoking. Jesus shares there will be (1) false Christs; (2) wars and rumors of; (3) famines, pestilences, and earthquakes; (4) tribulation for believers; (5) false prophets deceiving many; and (6) gospel proclamation in all the world to all the nations. We see these things happening, and Christians are being persecuted around the world, but their faith in these troubled areas is drawing more to Christ. With the help of David and SOM, even more are coming to faith, thus in alignment with Christ's sixth sign. As you read, you will sense an urgency and want to be a part of this incredible journey of harvesting souls for Christ.

—Ed White, *retired U.S. Naval Officer, state ambassador and Arizona State Task Force Director for Promise Keepers*

A *half-world away, India represents uncharted lands and vast, unlimited seas of peoples beyond imagination. David Witt has traveled the last decade to India and connected SOM International to experience opportunities few in America could have dreamed. His relationship with a bold Indian visionary leader – before ostracized but now deeply prized – is vital in the makings of an unforgettable movement of God. This is their amazing story, expressed in the lives of countless transformed lives.*

—Jeremiah Philip, *author and leadership coach*

A *great movement of God is happening in India, and this book shares personal stories of many of the people involved. Under persecution, poverty, and long travel distances with little transportation, the love of Jesus inspires these church planters to go and make disciples. Spirit of Martyrdom works from the States to help and encourage them; however, their stories have inspired me to work harder where I'm planted to help grow God's kingdom.*

—Laura Pratt, *pastor of The Gathering, Sedona*

David confirms what I've felt for a number of years now, particularly based on the stories I have heard from Iraq, Iran, Syria. It occurred to me how all those millennia ago, the first family of God, the family of Abraham, was split. Hagar was sent into the desert

with her son Ishmael, ostensibly to die. But God said no, he too would be a great nation. So what we see today is this family of Abraham being brought back together; the sons of Ishmael and the sons of Isaac are being reunited in Jesus, Messiah. What's truly mind-blowing is that this reunion is taking place in the same part of the world and today reaching into the Indian subcontinent. It's the story of God's family coming full circle. If that doesn't speak to eschatological questions, I don't know what does.

—Mark Dellinger, *Mishkan HaShofar*
Messianic Jewish Congregation

Revival is breaking out in India! For several years now, I have had the privilege of working alongside David Witt and Spirit of Martyrdom ministries by creating media pieces to help them communicate with their supporters. The true stories of widespread revival are amazing! This book captures some of the amazing work God is doing month after month as the gospel is penetrating India. You'll be encouraged to hear about lives transformed by the gospel and about Christians who are courageously living for Jesus in the midst of great persecution.

—Mark Stafford, *owner of Ablaze Media,*
www.ablaze.media

I was blessed to do some proofreading on this book, but I kept getting caught up reading it and would have to go back and make sure I didn't miss anything. If you have a heart to see people reached with the love of Jesus, this book will thrill you. If you are just interested in faith in Jesus, it will strengthen your convictions. You won't be able to stop reading it until you finish.

—Pastor Paul Wallace, Wayside Bible Chapel

If you want to read a story about perfect people with flawless theology entirely in agreement with your own, this book isn't for you. If you long to know about the continuing work of Jesus and his disciples told about in the book of Acts, breaking out through ordinary people hungry for truth and primed for joy—because, Lord have mercy, have they known grief—then this book will inspire you, not only to know about them but to join them.

—Raynna Myers, co-creator of The Martyrs' Cross and author of Beloved Prayers: A Martyrs' Cross Book of Prayers for the Persecuted

Thank you, David, for highlighting some modern examples of the principle laid out in the beginning of Genesis 1:28, "Then God blessed them, and God said to them, "Be fruitful and multiply; fill the earth and subdue it; ..." Multiplication has always been the plan

for God to fill the earth physically and then also to fill the earth spiritually.

I was encouraged and delighted to see God at work. I recommend this easy read to all who want to be reminded how God works through multiplication.

—Rob Nash, *missions pastor, Calvary Chapel, Vista, California*

After reading this book several times, I feel like calling it the Second Book of the Acts of the Apostles. Ok, maybe a bit of an exaggeration, but these stories emotionally connected with me. I am so thankful for dependency on the Holy Spirit, not our knowledge, to build institutional churches (hired hands – John 10) to be a channel of hope and blessings to everyone! Praise the Lord, he can use anyone and can find you from anywhere. Many blessings on everyone who reads this book and many testimonies of God's power!

—Saidou, *director of SOM Northwest Africa*

Every time I read the verses in 1 Thessalonians 1:2–3, I think of SOM International and David Witt and those sharing the gospel of our Lord and Savior around the world. We always thank God for you and continually mention you in our prayers. We remember before our God and Father your work produced by faith, your labor prompted by love, and your endurance inspired by hope in our Lord Jesus Christ. God chose you because

the gospel came to you not simply with words but also with the power of the Holy Spirit and deep conviction. God bless you, my brothers and sisters in Christ and all who read this book.

—**Sandy Houston,** businesswoman and
kingdom worker

David Witt and SOM have gifted the church in the West with a compelling collection of stories of radical obedience and extraordinary faith by "little people" from the church-planting movement in India. The testimonies of Peram, Kumar, and Tulasi have quickly become heroes of faith for me. Awakening in India shows us that church revival need not be encumbered by right resources, right strategies, and right programs; only a fierce dependence on the God who loves and sends is needed.

—**Tom Sharp,** Intervarsity Fellowship
director of study abroad

For More Books & Kingdom Resources:

Email: contact@SpiritofMartyrdom.com

Website:

spiritofmartyrdom.com/online-christian-bookstore/

For international orders, you may obtain our books at:

RansomPressInternational.com

Printed in the USA
CPSIA information can be obtained
at www.ICGtesting.com
CBHW030756051223
2355CB00003B/8